Editorial

»The nature of art is contrast«
Herbert Spencer 1820-1903

Black and white are every type designer's favourite contrast. The magic of typography unfolds in the balance between light and dark, loud and soft, thick strokes and fine hairlines.

The choice of contrast influences the legibility, mood and sometimes even the emotional impact of a font. That's why we have made fonts with high contrasts the theme of the 2025 calendar, which you can now study on many days.

Enjoy a whole year of changing typefaces from all over the world in our high-contrast calendar for a life between light and shadow - day and night!

Lars Harmsen & Raban Ruddigkeit

W0035933

TYPODARIUM

JANUARY

1

New Year's Day

Wednesday

YOU DON'T WANT TO BE BORED?

YOU WANT TO FEEL SOMETHING AS A PERSON?

Pina Neue, Display Sans, 2019,
Benedict Fromme & Lukas Ulonska, www.lukas-ulonska.webflow.io

Pina Neue

Berchtold's Day (CH)

RABBIT HOLE

Rabbit Hole, Display, 2023,
Tomasz Pawluk, www.instagram.com/boafff

TYPODARIUM

January

3

Friday

Mottek

Mottek, Sans, 2023,
Felix Fissenewert, www.felix.fissenewert.name

HAPPY BIRTHDAY T.

Lieferantenketensorgfaltspflichtengesetz

STOFFPREISGLEITKLAUSEL

Kühles Progressiönchen

Fünfzigjahrfeier | Desenrascanço

Donaldkacsázás | L'esprit de l'escalier

Házísárkány | Dalaæđa | Cigærpare

0 1 2 3 4 5 6 7 8 9

January

4

Saturday

LEKTORAT *OBLIQUE*

Lektorat Oblique, Text & Display, 2023,
Florian Fecher, www.type-together.com/lektorat-font

Extralight Light Regular

Semibold Bold

Extrabold

Black

TYPODARIUM

January

Sunday

Puffy

Puffy. Display. 2023,
Gaspar Muñoz, www.wtypefoundry.com

AaBbCcDdEeFf
GgHhIiJjKkLlMm
NnOoPpQqRr
SsTtUuVvXx
WwYyZz

TYPODARIUM

January ஜனவரி

Armenian Christmas Day (LB), Three Kings Day (PL), Epiphany

Monday திங்கள்

Kodai கோடை

Kodai, Display, 2024,
Sidharth Jaishankar, Ek Type, www.ektype.in

ஜில்லுனு ஒரு ஜிகர்தண்டா
புத்தம்புதிய SUPERHIT திரைப்படம்
catching some sun, riding some waves
Stylish-ஆன அராஜகம்

TYPODARIUM

January

Orthodox Christmas Day (RU)

Tuesday

DULCINEA SANS·

Dulcinea Sans, Sans, 2024,
John Vargar Beltrán, www.jvbfonts.co

Derived from the original **Dulcinea Serif** project of 2005, which that year commemorated the work Don Quixote, this is the Sans Serif version projected to an extensive typeface family with a total of 18 variations between weight and italics

HAIRLINE
THIN
LIGHT
REGULAR
MEDIUM
DEMI BOLD
BOLD
EXTRA BOLD
HEAVY

TYPODARIUM

January

8

Wednesday

Slandic

Slandic, Variable Script, 2020,
Philip Lammert, www.vibrant-types.com

Headlines Are Transformed Into Clear-Cut Messages With the Handwriting Type Family Slandic. Its Robust Appeal Combines the Elegance of Script Typefaces With the Lightness of Handwritten Notes. What Makes It So Playful Is the Synergy Between the Narrow Lowercase Letters and the Wide Capitals.

TYPODARIUM

January

Thursday

talk small

TT Neoris, Sans, 2023,
Typetype Foundry, www.typetype.org

TT Neoris

JANUARY

10

Friday

I did not anticipate waking up

Fresh word with wings

Murder Noodle

Charisma

Spektra, Sans, 2020,
Alja Herlah & Krista Likar, www.type-salon.com

Spektra

January

11

Saturday

Choose Life

Portobello Road Market

SIMPLEST

High STREET KENSINGTON

Great Branding

AW Conqueror Sans, Sans, 2022,
Jean François Porchez, www.typofonderie.com

AW Conqueror Sans

January

12

Sunday

PARGY

Ş.Þ.Q.R

Kudry, Serif, Sans & Stencil, 2023, A. Korolkova,
I. Chaeva, N. Nedashkovsky, www.paratype.com/fonts/pt/kudry

KUDRY

JANUARY

13

Coming of Age Day (JP)

Monday

Tatueté

Tatueté, Variable Serif, 2024,
Leopoldo Leal, www.pandemoniumtype.com

Tatueté Regular

Tatueté Semi Condensed

Tatueté Condensed

Tatueté Extra Condensed

Tatueté is a small animal whose body is covered with large bony scales and which rolls itself into a ball when it is attacked.

January

14

Tuesday

Grüezi

Grüezi, Sans, 2024,
Matej Vojtuš, Jozef Ondrik, www.regularlines.com

↓Kitzbühel↑
↳Hollernabfahrt↺
↱Hochfügen *Sölden*↵
Obertauern *Hochkönig*
Kreischberg Großarltal
↳Großglockner Kühtai↵
↓*Schmittenhöhe*↑

TYPODARIUM

January

15

Wednesday

HAL Colant Text

HAL Colant Text, Serif, 2023,
HAL Typefaces, type.hanli.eu

Drum & Bass
Hardstep
Speed Garage
'95 Jungle

TYPODARIUM

January

16

Thursday

Finador **Slab**

Finador Slab, Slab, 2019,
Julien Fincker, www.julienfincker.com

Thin *Oblique*
Extralight *Oblique*
Light *Oblique*
Regular *Oblique*
Medium *Oblique*
Bold *Oblique*
Black *Oblique*
Heavy *Oblique*

TYPODARIUM

January

17

Friday

— Pablo Neruda

"Love is born of memory, lives from intelligence and dies from forgetfulness."

Nuño, Display, 2024,
Gabriel Pulpo, www.pulpo.mx

Nuño

January

18

Saturday

Heidi Gallagher

Harrison Grant

Hannah Green

Harold Graham, Script, 2023,
Gulja Yeap, www.peachcreme.com

Harold Graham

January

Sunday

Burghì, Variable Display, 2023,
Alex Bossi & Fabrizio Falcone, CAST Foundry

Burghì

January

20

Martin Luther King Jr. Day (USA)

Monday

Super Castel

Super Castel, Serif, 2024,
Max Esnée, www.productiontype.com

Computer-Mediated Communication

Near Impenetrable Reconstruction

Institute For Analytic Journalism

Interrelationship Establishment

Unconventional Psychokinetic

Information Storage Systems

A like Aquarius
21 January - 19 February

Zodiac Alphabet

Zodiac Alphabet, Typo-Illustration, 2024,
Manuel Viergutz. www.TypoGraphicDesign.de

Manuel Viergutz is a
Graphic-Designer,
Type-Designer &
Lettering-Artist based
in Berlin. Founder of
the Font-Foundry
TypoGraphicDesign.de

TYPODARIUM

January

21

Tuesday

Kaio

Kaio, Variable Sans, 2023,
Romain Oudin, www.lift-type.fr

Six weights ↓ family ↓ Light Regular Medium Bold Black Super

JANUARY

22

WEDNESDAY

THIN INK

BOLD INK

Ink Trap Sans, Display Sans, 2024,
Manuel Viergutz, www.TypographicDesign.de

INK TRAP SANS

January

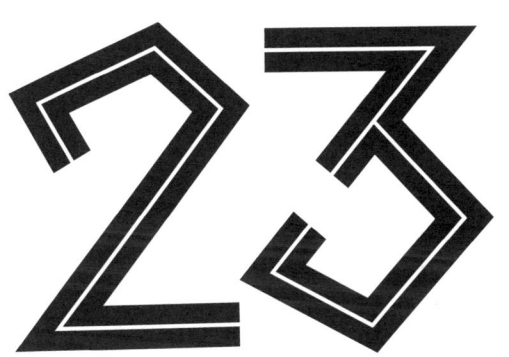

23

Thursday

RR-Lainer

RR-Lainer, Display, 2025,
Rafael Ramirez Lozano, BajioType, www.bajiotype.com

ABCDEFGHIJKLM
NÑOPQRSTUVW
XYZ1234567890
abcdefghijklmnñopqrstu
vwxyz.,:;¿?"#$%&/=+-@
*|¡!áéíóúÁÉÍÓÚ<>()[]{}«»
ÁáÉéÍíÓóÚúÜüÄäËëÏïÖöÜü

TYPODARIUM

January

24

Day of the Unification of the Romanian Principalities (RO)

Friday

Bata drum

Each bar is an idiophone tuned to a pitch of a musical scale

GLOCKENSPIEL

The modern western xylophone has bars of rosewood

Angklung

castanets & caxirola

Vocal, Sans, 2019, Anj Dimitrova, www.anjdimitrova.com

Vocal

January

25

Saturday

Mathilde

Mathilde, Serif, 2024,
Mara Nolze, www.sudtipos.com

»**Unter** *allen* ABER
schien! **Mathilde***
78% *die* {Rosen} *am*
MEISTEN? &–[zu]
;) lieben (…) 210.«

TYPODARIUM

January

26

Australia Day (AU), Republic Day (IN)

Sunday

BEHOLDEN

Evangelicals

PENITENCE

Reverberant

OVERLONG

Visconte, Display, 2023,
Andrea Tartarelli, www.zetafonts.com

Visconte

January

27

Monday

Afical Neue

Afical Neue, Neo Grotesk, 2019.
Deni Anggara, www.formatypefoundry.com

MODULE SYSTEM

JET-45 ✈ 18:20 WIB

Int'l Airport USA

New ⇄ Format©21

Visuell Grafik 1957

H.E.X Studio RC

TYPODARIUM

JANUARY

28

Seollal (KR)

TUESDAY

TUPLET

Tuplet, Serif Mono, 2023,
Jakob Fangmeier, www.futurefonts.xyz, www.type.design

A *DuoSpace* Typeface with Caps in TWO (2) widths! *WOW* this opens ↯ entirely new ways of *typesetting.* ~www.futurefonts.xyz

JANUARY

29

Chineses New Year (Spring Festival) (CN,ID,MY), Seollal (KR),
Tet (Lunar New Year) (VN)

Wednesday

@?!¡£$†

0123456789

Uu Vv Ww Xx Yy Zz

Kk Ll Mm Nn Oo Pp Qq Rr Ss Tt

Aa Bb Cc Dd Ee Ff Gg Hh Ii Jj

Adam Greasley, www.cottypeco.com

Cribin, Serif, 2023.

CRIBIN

JANUARY

30

Seollal (KR)

THURSDAY

BOKAJ

Bokaj, Display, 2023,
Zusanna Gruszczynaska, www.instagram.com/zuzanna.elea

SEAMLESSLY FUSES VINTAGE CHARM WITH CONTEMPORARY ELEGANCE

VINTAGE SOPHISTICATION

A B C D E F G H I J K L M
N O P Q R S T U V W X Y
ZUZANNAELEA

TYPODARIUM

JANUARY

31

FRIDAY

HAPPY BIRTHDAY, SWEETHEART

CHEERS TO YOU
FOR ANOTHER TRIP
AROUND THE SUN!

Amboni, Display, 2023,
Anita Jürgeleit, www.typefthis.studio

AMBONI

FEBRUARY

SATURDAY

THE BLUE POT

The Blue Pot, Display, 2025,
Hunger & Koch × Sebastian Moock, www.sebastianmoock.de

FOODPRINT IS GOOD
MEMORIES. NOM, NOM, NOM.

TYPODARIUM

February

2

Sunday

Gigafly

Gigafly, Display, 2023,
Roch Modrzejewski, www.rohhtype.com

EXTRABØLD

HⱰ QUALITY

a b c d e f g h i
j k l m n o p q
r s t u v w x y z

TYPODARIUM

Februrary

3

Constitution Day (MX)

Monday

CA Yoshiro Wide

CA Yoshiro Wide, Variable, 2023,
Thomas Schostok, www.cape-arcona.com

EXPLORING
NEW
↳WORLDS
CAN BE FUN!
19374 ⊠ 05268

TYPODARIUM

FEBRUARY

TUESDAY

ZANCO

Zanco, Variable, 2024,
In-House, www.weareinhouse.com

BOLD &THIN

TYPODARIUM

foburary

wednesday

spiral

Spiral, Variable Display, 2024,
Jacob Wise, www.wisetype.nl

druids
flagship
greece
sloop

TYPODARIUM

February

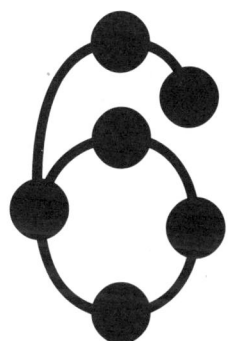

Thursday

WF Node

WF Node, Variable Display, 2024,
Marinus Klinksik, www.marinusklinksik.de

Strictly Dancefloor Business!

TYPODARIUM

February

7

Friday

Amilia_v2

Amilia_v2, Sans, 2024,
David Henni Wiesner, www.davidwiesner.de

→Elina←

»Look, I'm all for change. But, do we really need to add high contrasts to every typeface, just to avoid creating more Helvetica clones?«

→Amilia←

»Well, I'd say yes.«

TYPODARIUM

February

8

Prešeren Day (Cultural Day) (SI)

Saturday

Whale

Whale, Mono, 2022,
Pieter van Rosmalen, www.caketype.com

"Elettricitá
ℂHefðarmaður
składających
flächenmäßig
Acceptgiro's
gudžarátský"

TYPODARIUM

FEBRUARY

St. Maroun's Day (LB)

SUNDAY

ART NOUVEAU & STEAM PUNK

SOMETHING BETWEEN

EYE-CATCHER HEADLINES

Sveava Stencil, Display, 2023,
Andreas Seidel, www.astype.de, fontstore.astype.com

SVEVA STENCIL

FEBRUARY

10

MONDAY

HOUGAN

Hougan, Japanese Display, 2025,
Shintaro Ajioka, www.font.jpn.com

真にローカルなものだけが
インターナショナルに来り得る。
真のオリジナルは
自らの足元から生まれるもの。

Only what is truly local can
become international.
The real originality comes
from your own place.

TYPODARIUM

February

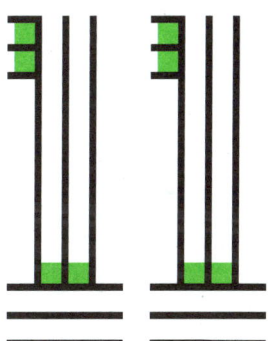

11

National Foundation Day (JP)

Tuesday

rîbîn

Rîbîn, Display, 2024,
Paul Bokstag, www.paulbokstag.com

westerday

TYPODARIUM

February

12

Wednesday

ROULADE

Roulade, Display, 2023,
Romain Diant, www.asenso.fr

Lean forward while pushing on your feet and legs, to drive your hips over your head, while your hands remain glued to the floor. Your arms and legs should straighten while remaining slightly bent, as you roll forward and land on your back.

IN ROULADE WE TRUST

February

Thursday

Unigeo

Unigeo, Sans, 2023, Cosimo Lorenzo Pancini,
Francesco Canovaro, Andrea Tartarelli, www.zetafonts.com

GHOSTBUSTER
workhorse sans
Modularity
1980"s

TYPODARIUM

February

friday

Burns

Burns, Sans, 2023,
Nolan Paparelli, www.nolan-paparelli.ch

Happy Valentine's day!

TYPODARIUM

February

15

Saturday

弘德隶书

Hongde Lishu Family, Modern Clerical Script, 2024,
Li Ying & Zhan Goudong, www.hanyi.com.cn/

祝典舞

承慈福

光

煎矮慈元书写外

乃厅计队比厄酬

儿女义工小义及

TYPODARIUM

February

15

Sunday

TYPODARIUM

Thousand

demographic

Southern

Hemisphères

Berlin, Variable Display, 2023,
Roman Seban, www.205.tf

Berlin

february

Family Day (CA), Presidents' Day (USA)

MONDAY

MMM, Display, 2021,
André Toet, www.andretoet.com

Good Design Is All About Making Other Designers Feel Like Idiots Because That Idea Wasn't Theirs.

Frank Chimero

TYPODARIUM

February

18

Tuesday

Rybaczka

Rybaczka, Sans, 2024,
Roman Wilhelm, www.romantype.net

Rybaczka means fisherwoman in Polish. Lody, gofry, plaża, pierogi leniwe, piwo jasne, Pomorze Zachodnie, ul. Rybacki, 2024.

TYPODARIUM

February

19

Wednesday

APK Narrative

APK Narrative, Sans, 2024,
Autograph Peter Korsman, www.apk-type.com

Default

The Story Is Always Changing.

Set 01

The Story Is Always Changing.

TYPODARIUM

P like Pisces
20 February - 20 March

Zodiac Alphabet

Zodiac Alphabet, Typo-Illustration, 2024,
Manuel Viergutz, www.TypoGraphicDesign.de

Manuel Viergutz is a Graphic-Designer, Type-Designer & Lettering-Artist based in Berlin. Founder of the Font-Foundry TypoGraphicDesign.de

TYPODARIUM

February

20

Thursday

Evert

Evert, Sans, 2024,
Kostas Bartsokas, www.foundryfivetype.com/evert-greek

Evert is a typeface that breaks the mould while respectfully nodding to its classic roots. Like a themed rollercoaster it invites you on a ride over the plains of the early grotesques, into the tunnels of mechanical essence, up on the hills of the experimental, and over the district of contemporary modernity. This clearly isn't your grandma's typeface!

TYPODARIUM

FEBRUARY

21

FRIDAY

GABRIELLE

Gabrielle, Serif, 2023,
Charlene Sepentzis, www.charlies.ca

JE SOUHAITE
UN CORPS AUDACIEUX
DES ÉTÉS DE CHEVEUX MOUILLÉS
UNE MULTITUDE DE DÉJEUNERS
JE COHABITE
AVEC L'ADVERSAIRE
POUR TENIR TES MITAINES
PORTER TON SAC À DOS

TYPODARIUM

February

22

Saturday

Junge Kunst

Junge Kunst, Sans, 2024,
Benjamin Paul Knopper & Jan Eloy Gabriel, www.zickzaq.com

aaa

One day I killed my squirrel. I did it voluntarily, and joy picked trough my eyes. The zebra in my basement was flabbergasted and toxic.

TYPODARIUM

February

23

The Emperor's Birthday (JP)

Sunday

Hetskelet

Hetskelet, Display, 2024,
Sophia Tai, www.sophiatai.com

muscle and bones

inline

curious kontrast

morbid modulation

TYPODARIUM

FEBRUARY

Independence Day (EE)

THE ETERNAL IDOL

The Eternal Idol, Display, 2023,
Mattia Luise, Ariel Brandolini, www.design-associati.it

RISE UP TO THE SHINING

?#{}@&$¢€Ø%
ÆŒ0123456789

TYPODARIUM

February

25

Tuesday

Foundry Unie

Foundry Unie, Sans, 2022,
David Quay, Stuart de Rozario, www.thefoundrytypes.com

Geometric Appearance

Calmly *Understated*

Modernist *Movement*

Universal *Application*

Ubiquitous *Beauty*

Sympathetic *Shapes*

TYPODARIUM

February

26

WEDNESDAY

Pasticcino

Pasticcino, Serif, 2021,
Dafne Matínez, www.cocijotype.com

Pasticcino

ARTESANÍAS EN LACA

Elegant & Tide

High contrast / **Bold body**

A MILLION MILES AWAY ☞ OLD & MODERN

same recipe from 1967: 235 grs. of flour / 4 eggs / lots of love!

TYPODARIUM

February

27

THURSDAY

NAVE

Nave, Serif, 2024,
Jamie Clarke, www.jamieclarketype.com

Exemplification
Impressiveness
Transcendence
Representation
Misunderstood
Confidentiality
Sentimentalist

TYPODARIUM

February

28

Friday

Quietism

Quietism, Serif, 2022,
Michael Rafailyk, www.michaelrafailyk.com

Quietism is the name given
(especially in Catholic theology)
to a set of contemplative practices
that rose in popularity in France,
Italy, and Spain during the late
1670ˢ and 1680ˢ, *particularly
associated with the writings of the
Spanish mystic Miguel de Molinos*

TYPODARIUM

March

1

Independence Movement Day (KR)

Saturday

Curly Pixie
Bouncy Curls
Curly Fringe
Side Curls
Micro Curls

Cacao Grotesk, Sans, 2024,
Christian Lindemann, www.t-a-n-d-e-m.eu

Cacao Grotesk

MARCH

2

SUNDAY

ᚖ67890123456789ᚖ

MONOLINE & CONTRAST
•FAMILY•
•INSPIRED•TYPE•

VIENNESE SECESSION

Exentrica, Display, 2023,
Nick Cooke, www.g-type.com

EXENTRICA

MARCH

3

Liberation Day (BG),
Carnival Monday/Mardi Gras (AR, BR, UR)

MONDAY

AW CONQUEROR STINCILLA

AW Conqueror Stincilla, Display, 2022,
Jean François Porchez, www.typofonderie.com

FLORALIES

TURBULL & STOCKDALE LTD

DECORATIVE ART

CRYSTAL

SIMPSON&GODLEE

TYPODARIUM

March

4

Carnival Tuesday/ Mardi Gras (AR, BR, PT, UR)

Tuesday

Rooftop Extra

Rooftop Wide

Rooftop Normal

Rooftop Compact

Rooftop Condesed

Rooftop Ultra Condensed

Rooftop, Sans, 2024,
Interval Type, www.intervaltype.com

Rooftop

March

5

Wednesday

mr gabe

Mr Gabe, Serif, 2022,
Andrea Leksen, www.leksendesign.com

Tango orchestra accompanied by bandoneón

BACKWARD ✱ OCHOS

Nostalgia, sadness, laments for lost love

lucky ✱ shoes

CANARO D'ARIENZO DI SARLI PUGLIESE PIAZZOLLA

🐦 March 🐦

6

🐦 Thursday 🐦

Routine, Sans, 2023,
Frederick Wiltshire, www.blazetype.eu

ROUTINE

March

مارس

7

الجمعة   Friday

29LT Azahar AL Text & Display

29LT Azahar AL Text & Display, Variable Display Serif, 2024,
José Carratala [Latin] & Naïma Ben Ayed [Arabic], www.29LT.com

الإِبْهارِ البَصَرِيِّ لِلْصُورَةِ أَوِ الخِدَعِ

TYPODARIUM

MARCH

International Women's Day (RU)

SATURDAY

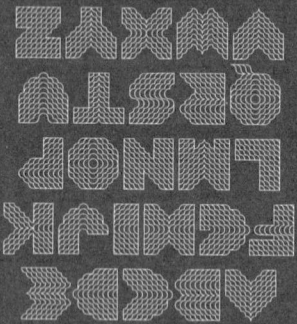

ABCDE
FGHIJK
LMNOP
QRSTU
VWXYZ

Patroon Display, 2023,
Paul Bokslag, www.paulbokslag.com

PATROON

March

Sunday

N

ABCDEFGHIJKLMN
OPQRSTUVWXYZ
abcdefghijklmno
pqrstuvwxyz?!;*&
0123456789#$%

Sahla

Sahla, Stencil, 2023,
Alanna Munro, www.alannamunro.com

March

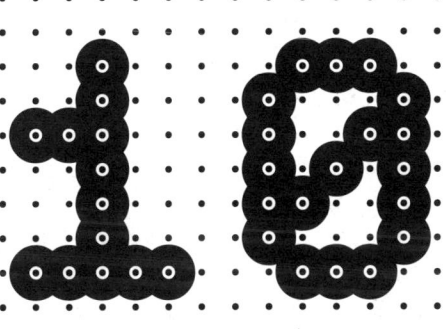

MONDAY

ALT/REG-000
ModuL↔(AR)
File:848_KB
Dot_Matrix_

Atexa Mono, Display, 2023,
Radinal Riki Mutaqin, www.atktype.gumroad.com

Atexa Mono

March માર્ચ

11th

Tuesday મંગળવારે

TYPODARIUM

NAATAK FAMILY

Naatak Family, Script, 2024,
Multiple Designers, www.ektype.in/naatak

MARCH

12

Wednesday

Buwaya

Buwaya, Display Sans, 2024,
Lukas Ulonska, www.instagram.com/lukasulonska

MAG-INGAT!

taong umiiyak na parang buwaya, masamang intensiyon sa ilalim ng kanilang pagluha!

March

13

Thursday

Matryo

Matryo, Sans, 2023,
Michael Parson, www.typogama.com

Matryo is a multilingual typeface family that covers all Latin, Cyrillic & Greek languages. Available in six weights with italics.

typography	**τυπογραφία**	**типографія**
typography	τυπογραφία	типографія
typography	τυπογραφία	типографія
typography	τυπογραφία	типографія
typography	τυπογραφία	типографія
typography	τυπογραφία	типографія
typography	τυπογραφία	типографія

TYPODARIUM

MARCH

Holi (IN)

FRIDAY

TWISTA SHADING

TWISTA INNER

TWISTA BACKGROUND

TWISTA SHADED

TWISTA OUTLINE

TWISTA OPEN LINE

Twista, Display, 2023,
Viktor Nübel, www.viktornuebel.com

TWISTA

March

15

Saturday

Uggla Sans

Uggla Sans, Sans, 2024,
Hanspeter Lobis, www.typografie.it

Important facts about owls

There are no owls in Antarctica.

TYPODARIUM

March

16

Sunday

PITAHAYA

Pitahaya, Sans, 2024,
Manuel Corradine & Víctor Gómez, www.laletreria.co

*following the clean forms of «grotèsque sans», *with* unusual *cuts* & styles. Inspired by the {tropical} *fruits* of Låtin América!!!

TYPODARIUM

March

17

Benito Juárez Day (MX)

Monday

CT Selector

CT Selector, Variable Sans, 2024,
Robert Finkei, www.contextype.com

ABCD... and more!

Collection of typefaces for everyday use at contextype.com

TYPODARIUM

March

18

Tuesday

Honest

Honest, Display Serif, 2023,
Diego Aravena Silo, www.wtypefoundry.com

Thin *Thin*
Light *Light*
Regular *Italic*
Medium *Medium*
Bold ***Bold***
Black ***Black***
Heavy ***Heavy***

TYPODARIUM

MARCH

19

Saint Joseph's Day (CO)

Wednesday

HÆTTI

Hætti, Variable Display, 2024,
Gregor Maria Sahl, www.gregormaria.com

BAAaCCFDEe
GGHJJKLMM
NNOPRRrTS
UYIXWZ!

aabccdegg
himjknlopq
rffswtttxyz

ZUERICH

TYPODARIUM

MARCH

20

Thursday

Gregory Grotesk

Gregory Grotesk, Variable Sans, 2024,
Jakob Runge, www.TypeMates.com

Weird and wonderful

cosy vibes for a progressively nostalgic audience

refresh your sans serifed workflow

INKED GROTESK

Not usual, not even normal, but amazing. ✳ Probably.

TYPODARIUM

A like Aries
21 March - 20 April

Zodiac Alphabet

Zodiac Alphabet, Typo-Illustration, 2024,
Manuel Viergutz, www.TypoGraphicDesign.de

Manuel Viergutz is a
Graphic-Designer,
Type-Designer &
Lettering-Artist based
in Berlin. Founder of
the Font-Foundry
TypoGraphicDesign.de

TYPODARIUM

MARCH

FRIDAY

ANOREXIA

ANOREXIA, Display, 2011,
Bonez Designz, www.bonezdesignz.com

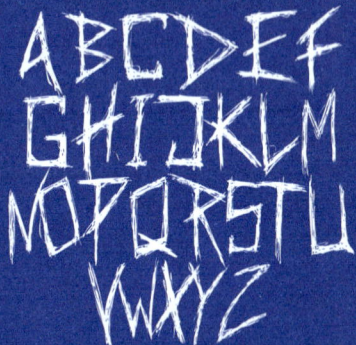

TYPODARIUM

MARCH

22

SATURDAY

HÓLÓS

Holos, Display Serif, 2023,
Alyona Korysta, www.behance.net/alyonakorysta

HÓLÓS /VÓÌCE/
←ÌS ÀN UKKAÌNÌAN→
↖FÓNT↗
ÌNSPÌKED KY
[PÀVLÓ KÓVZHUN]
(1896–1939)
©WÓKKS

TYPODARIUM

March

23

Sunday

BD LoFi UCX

BD LoFi, Variable Display, 1997/2023,
Lopetz, Büro Destruct, www.typedifferent.com

BD Lo-Fi™
was originally
designed on
an Amiga #1200
in 1997.☼田口◇◆☀°©®
→ Extended and
converted into
a variable UFX-FONT
in #2023 on
the AXIS_WHEIGHT

TYPODARIUM

March

24

Monday

HARBER

Harber, Display, 2023,
Benoît Bodhuin, www.bb-bureau.fr

HARBER is designed of dots on a grid. Letters are invariable, only dots change, parameterized by five axis: weight, slant, volume, noise and optical size.

TYPODARIUM

MARCH

25

Independence Day (GR)

TUESDAY

Picaresk

Picaresk, Sans, 2023,
Rui Abreu, www.r-typography.com

Failed Seriousness

Failed Seriousness

Failed Seriousness

Failed Seriousness

Failed Seriousness

Failed Seriousness

TYPODARIUM

March

26

Wednesday

© **Typographic Systems™**

MÄRGÏÑÄĽŠPALÈ

FESTIVAL DE LA MUSIQUE

149th Street NEW YORK

Eloquent

Piece of Nature

CONTEMPORARY ART & CULTURE

Flavoure, Display, 2023,
Christoph Uherr, www.jpfonts.com

Flavoure

March

27

Thursday

SIMON

Simon, Serif, 2013–2024, K. Radoeva,
D. Golub, A. Lubovenko www.paratype.com/fonts/pt/simon

S·P·Q·R

SIMON IS A REVIVAL of typefaces by
French punchcutter of the 1st half of the
16th century, *Simon de Colines*. Simon
includes upright and italic faces in three
optical sizes. It is a soft and relaxed garalde,
very well suited for book design.

TYPODARIUM

March

28

Friday

OTC Riga

OTC Riga, Slab, 2019,
Ograda Type Company, www.ograda.co

"Again the blackbirds
sings; the streams
Wake, laughing, from
their winter dreams,
And tremble in the
April showers
The tassels of the
maple flowers [...]"

TYPODARIUM

March

29

Nyepi (Day of Silence) (ID)

SATURDAY

Ease Family

Ease Family, Variable, 2023,
Felix Pfäffli, Robin Eberwein, www.fonts.studiofeixen.ch

Ease–[1]Standard
[2](Semi)Rounded[3]
[4]DoubleRounded
[5]FullRounded
[6]SemiDisplay
[7]Display
[8]Geometric (A+B)

MARCH

30

Eid al-Fitr (TR, ID, LB)

SUNDAY

LEFT WEEKS NINE THIRTY

Rukh, Display, 2024,
Kaamkaaj, www.kaamkaaj.work

RUKH

MARCH

31

Hari Raya Puasa (MY)

MONDAY

PASTO

Pasto, Display, 2019,
Julia Martinez Diana, www.antipixel.com.ar

CHIỀU. SKETCH!
ALMOND 'SOX
WHO? LAWLESS

TYPODARIUM

April

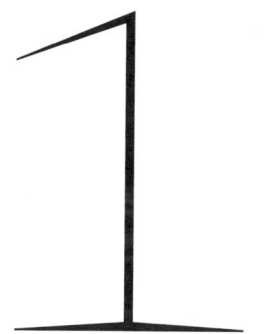

1

Hari Raya Puasa (PL)

Tuesday

Oxymora Mono

Oxymora Mono, Display Mono, 2024,
Lucas Guizetti, www.lucasguizetti.cargo.site

April

2

Malvinas Day (AR)

Wednesday

Phono

Phono, Variable, 2022,
Paul Eslage, phono.pauleslage.de

The Face of Type

The Sound of Speech

TYPODARIUM

April

3

Thursday

APK Monogami

APK Monogami, Mono Display Grotesque, 2017/2024,
Autograph Peter Korsman, www.apk-type.com

{26/30] pts.
>:Default
>;Alternate/
>;Alternate

TYPODARIUM

April

4

Friday

Chutz

Chutz, Display Serif, 2023,
Michael Rafaljuk, www.michaelrafaljuk.com

Regular
Medium
Bold
Black

TYPODARIUM

April

5

Qingming Festival (Tomb-Sweeping Day) (CN)

Saturday

Playground Script

PP Playground Script, Script, 2024,
Francesca Bolognini & Mat Desjardins, www.pangrampangram.com

Play is the Highest Form of Research!

TYPODARIUM

APRIL

SUNDAY

WITTMANN DISPLAY VIVIT

Wittmann Display Vivit, Display, 2022,
Mona Franz, www.justyourtype.de

TODAY IS FOR MAKING THE DIFFERENCE

TYPODARIUM

April

7

Hung Kings Commemorations Day (VN)

Monday

Architype Motherwell

Architype Motherwell, Display Stencil, 2024,
W. Crouwel, D. Quay, S. de Rozario, www.thefoundrytypes.com

Geometric Sequence Configuration

Modular Mathematical System

Sculptural Infrastructure

Stedelijk Museum

Integrated Symmetry

TYPODARIUM

APRIL

8

Tuesday

CTCO HOPPS

CTCO Hopps, Display Sans, 2023,
Adam Greasley, www.colttypeco.com

Soft

Aa Bb Cc Dd Ee Ff Gg Hh Ii Jj Kk Ll
Mm Nn Oo Pp Qq Rr Ss Tt Uu Vv Ww
Xx Yy Zz 0 1 2 3 4 5 6 7 8 9 ? ! & £ $

Regular

Aa Bb Cc Dd Ee Ff Gg Hh Ii Jj Kk Ll
Mm Nn Oo Pp Qq Rr Ss Tt Uu Vv Ww
Xx Yy Zz 0 1 2 3 4 5 6 7 8 9 ? ! & £ $

TYPODARIUM

April

9

Wednesday

Kefa III

Kefa III, Slab, 2024,
Jérémie Hornus & Gaëtan Baehr, www.black-foundry.com

Latin & Ethiopic

ብርቄካንማ ቡና
ሁለት ሺ ሁለት አስራ ሦስት
Kaffa, Ethiopia
inspired by Ethiopic
calligraphy

TYPODARIUM

APRIL

10

THURSDAY

AMBERWOOD

Amberwood, Display, 2023,
Alanna Munro, www.alannamunro.com

EXTRA LIGHT FOREST EXTRA LIGHT
LIGHT FOREST LIGHT FOREST LIGHT
REGULAR FOREST REGULAR
SEMIBOLD FOREST SEMIBOLD
BOLD FOREST BOLD FOREST

TYPODARIUM

APRIL

11

FRIDAY

GENERATION MONO

Generation Mono, Display, 2020,
Nguyen Gobber, www.nguyengobber.com

ON
PE
EX
NT

TYPODARIUM

April

Saturday

Psyleidoscope

Psyleidoscope, Serif Display, 2023,
Markus Strümpel, www.designpiraten.com

One pill makes you

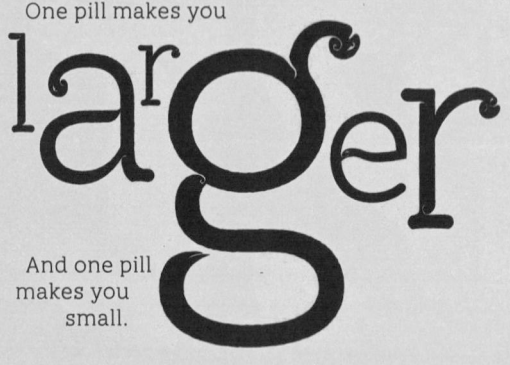

And one pill
makes you
small.

TYPODARIUM

APRIL

13

SUNDAY

ZACHEL

Zachel, Display, 2024,
Felix Fissenewert, www.felix.fissenewert.name

HIGH CONTRAST
GROßKLEINEMACHEN
FÜNFZIGJAHREFIX
DESENRASCANÇO
HÁZISÁRKÁNY 012345
6789 DALALÆDA
unicase @x%

TYPODARIUM

April

14

Monday

HAL Repost

HAL Repost, Slab, 2024,
HAL Typefaces, type.hanli.eu

Repost is a friendly, monolinear slab serif with rounded terminal endings. Inspired by ATF's Post Monotone No. 2, originally designed in 1903 for the Saturday Evening Post, Repost's stylistic extension includes Regular, *Regular Italic*, Mono and *Mono Italic*.

TYPODARIUM

APRIL

15

Tuesday

Aiglon

Aiglon, Sans, 2022,
Jean François Porchez, www.typofonderie.com

LIBERTY

Avenue des Champs-Élysées

République

IT IS FORBIDDEN TO PROHIBIT

Louis de Funès

TYPODARIUM

April

15

Wednesday

Pixie

Pixie, Display, 2024,
Natalie Giesel, nataliegiesel.de

SCHMETTERLING
schmetterling

TYPODARIUM

April

17

Maundy Thursday

Thursday

Right Serif Mono

Right Serif Mono, Variable Serif Mono, 2023,
Alex Slobzheninov, www.slobzheninov.com

About 57% {not ⅔}
Prïnt & Leave co®
#lichrally £10.99
02«ßñ"ʊ‡™Łŀŀøɟůŋð№
↓Return if found↑
Since *old-style*
has been a thing!

TYPODARIUM

April

18

Good Friday

Friday

Buvard

Buvard, Serif, 2024,
Max Esnée, www.max-esnee.com

Filmore East, 1970
"$20 Fine" — 4:59
Crash Landing [34]
{9} *If Six Was Nine*
Crosstown Traffic*

TYPODARIUM

APRIL

19

SATURDAY

VELOCITY

Velocity, Display, 2024,
Paul Hanslow with Kaja Słojewska, www.tandemtype.co

DROPOUT DRAFTING
VÉLODROME
FAIRE L'ÉLASTIQUE
WHEELSUCKER
GROUPE DE TÊTE

TYPODARIUM

APRIL

Easter Sunday

REGATO

Regato, Script, 2014, Ewen Prigent,
www.myfonts.com/collections/regato-font-la-boite-graphique

REGATO IS A HAND MADE FONT IDEAL FOR YOUR GRAPHIC PROJECT. USAGE RECOMMENDATIONS : TITLE, SHORT TEXT, CHILDREN'S BOOK, POSTER, BOOK COVER, BROCHURE, LABEL, MAGAZINE

TYPODARIUM

T like Taurus
21 April - 20 May

Zodiac Alphabet

Zodiac Alphabet, Typo-Illustration, 2024,
Manuel Viergutz, www.TypoGraphicDesign.de

Manuel Viergutz is a
Graphic-Designer,
Type-Designer &
Lettering-Artist based
in Berlin. Founder of
the Font-Foundry
TypoGraphicDesign.de

April

21

Easter Monday, Tiradentes Day (BR)

Monday

Sharp Earth

Sharp Earth, Sans, 2024, Lukas Sharp, My-Lan Thuong, Jovana Jocic & Chris Hernández (Latin), Maha Akl & Shad El-Sabbagh (Arabic), Cadson Demak (Thai), Anagha Narayanan (Devanagari), Calvin Kwok, Klio Peng, Wei-Yun Kan, Fang-Ping Lin & Kazuhiro Yamada (Japanese), REALTYPE, Inc. & Connor Davenport (mastering), www.sharptype.co

สภาพอากาศ *Tετυ wευ yɔ*

Hệ Mặt Trời 宇宙プラズマ

प्राकृतिकसूची *Kлиматолог*

Γεωγραφία 温室効果ガス

استوائية بحيرة *ภาวะโลกร้อน*

Exploration 赤道面の傾き

TYPODARIUM

April

22

Tuesday

VILLA

Villa, Serif, 2024,
Ricardo Santos, www.vanarchiv.com

ABCDEFGHIJKLMN
OPQRSTUVWXYZ
0123456789 abcdefg
hijklmnopqrstuvw
xyz 0123456789 !?*§:,
%@(){}[]$€£¥ßœ‡†

TYPODARIUM

April

23

National Sovereignty and Children's Day (TR)

Wednesday

Profumo

Profumo, Sans, 2024,
Emmanuel Besse, www.productiontype.com

Anthropomorphism	**BIOSIGNATURES**
Plant Identification	**HEAT OF FUSION**
Socratea Exorrhiza	**INCANDESCENCE**
Urban Exploration	**MOUNT EVEREST**
Lateral Meristems	ABSTRACTIONIST
Megasporangium	PHOTOREALISTIC
Boscia Albitrunca	CONRAD GESNER
Ancient Egyptian	RANUNCULACEAE
Portrait Painting	THERMODYNAMIC

TYPODARIUM

April

24

Thursday

Tapir

Tapir, Display, 2022,
Hannes von Döhren, www.hvdfonts.com

Clean

Extra Cheese

Tripple Full House Patty Combo

TYPODARIUM

April

25

Anzac Day (AU), Liberation Day (IT)

Friday

Telka

Telka, Sans, 2023,
Jan Weidemüller, www.ultra-kuhl.com

MULBERRY KOTI

MPP 60–250 SP^1 LDN
SAINT GOBLIN
DOT   F37 / M80 AI
FE---00074 🍦®

₿●●●●●●™

TYPODARIUM

APRIL

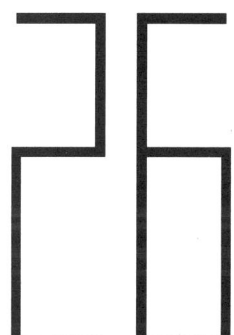

King's Day (NL)

SATURDAY

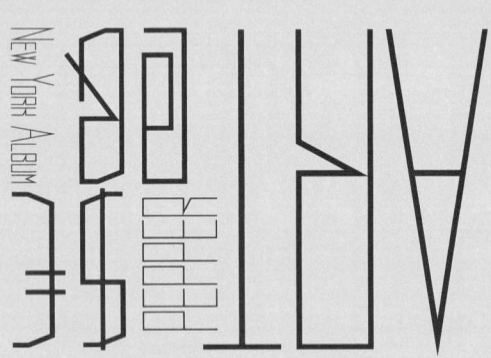

New York Album, Display, 2023,
Mattia Luise, Ariel Brandolini, www.design-associati.it

APRIL

27

SUNDAY

MGZebra

MGZebra, Display, 2022,
Monika Gause, www.vektorgarten.de

a typeface like a
maze! az cdef ghijkl
mnopqrstuvwxyz
äöüß ijk ä tarcmgff
1234567890 & * @ ? ¨ '¨'
ßarmomogijvjy

TYPODARIUM

APRIL

28

MONDAY

VTG STENCIL IDEAL No.1

VTG Stencil Ideal No.1, Stencil, 2023,
Andreas Seidel, www.astype.de, fontstore.astype.com

A TRADITIONAL STENCIL
TYPEFACE FOR MARKING,
SINCE 1913.
DESIGNED FROM AN EARLY
ONE-INCH IDEAL STENCIL
CUTTING MACHINE.

TYPODARIUM

APRIL

29

Showa Day (JP)

TUESDAY

DOUBLEBASS

DoubleBass, Display, 2018,
Cosimo Lorenzo Pancini, www.zetafonts.com

ANATOMY OF A MURDER

ENTERTAINMENT

SPARTACUS

THE VICTORS

TYPODARIUM

APRIL

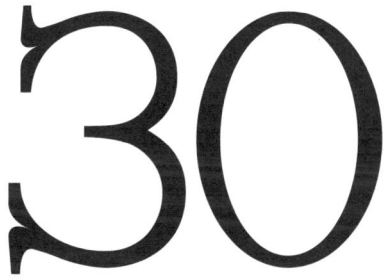

30

Reunification Day (VN)

WEDNESDAY

ROMANCE

Romance, Display, 2023,
Charlene Sepentzis, www.charlies.ca

JE SUIS ÉMUE DEVANT
AUTANT DE ROUGE;
ON DIRAIT DU VELOURS,
ON DIRAIT DE LA FORCE,
ON DIRAIT LA VRAIE VIE.
JE ME DEMANDE
SI J'AI BESOIN
DES HOMMES POUR
ÊTRE HEUREUSE

☙

TYPODARIUM

May

International Labour Day

Thursday

Adapt & Adapt Variable

Adapt, Sans, 2021, Prof. Jürgen Huber & Martin Wenzel,
supertype®, www.supertype.de/fonts/adapt

Aa Bb Cc Dd Ee Ff Ggg Hh Ii Jj
Kk Lll Mm Nn Oo Pp Qq Rr Ss Tt
Uu Vv Ww Xx Yy Zz · 12 34 56
78 90 → €¥ ○# &@ ?! 12 ¾]•}·)

8 WEIGHTS & VARIABLE

Thin Light Semilight Regular
Medium **Bold** **Extrabold** **Black**

5 WIDTHS & VARIABLE

Compressed Compact Condensed Narrow **Normal**

TYPODARIUM

May

2

Friday

Gimbo

Gimbo, Display Sans, 2023,
Deni Anggara, www.halbfett.com

@Mail
детский
клуб

Big-size
Lemon

TYPODARIUM

may

3

Constitution Memorial Day (JP), Constitution Day (PL)

saturday

exhibitions typeface
cybernetische grids
edited indoctrinations
creacad voornaggen
fernhout landschap

Fernhout, Display Stencil, 2021,
W. Crouwel, D. Quay, S. de Rozario, www.thefoundrytypes.com

Fernhout

May

Greenery Day (JP), Martyrs' Day (LB)

AMBIDEXTER

Ambidexter, Display, 2021,
Egor Belozerov, www.paratype.com/fonts/eb/abidexter

CONTR *Free*
OVER SIAL
SIAL OVER
CONTR *Free*

TYPODARIUM

MAY

5

Early May Bank Holiday (GB), Children's Day (JP, KR),
Liberation Day (NL), Buddha's Birthday

monday

OTC Topo

OTC Topo, Display, 2024,
Ograda Type Company, www.ograda.co

În scaunul din stânga, cu ochii la reperele de identificare dar și la harta «topo» pe care...

TYPODARIUM

May

6

Saint George's Day (BG)

Tuesday

PoW Garnier

PoW Garnier, Serif, 2024,
Fanny Hamelin, www.proof-of-words.com

Tighten **CROW**

Bleaker LEAPS

Filched STALK

Rawest POKES

Edison GRIME

TYPODARIUM

MAY

7

WEDNESDAY

HOUR

Hour, Variable Display, 2023,
Federico Parra Barrios, www.205.tf

AIR
TIME
SIX

TYPODARIUM

May

8

Liberation Day (CZ)

THURSDAY

Latino Gothic®

Latino Gothic, Sans, 2023,
Alfonso García, www.latinotype.com

Original 7" 45 RPM
The First Nine Years,
Box Set: B9R050.
Bridge Nine Records.
Latinotype Classic™
@South America.

May

9

Victory Day (RU)

Friday

Basil Lime Margarita

Basil Lime Magarita, Script, 2023,
Gulya Yeap, www.peachcreme.com

A zesty quick brown fox jumps over the lazy dog. sipping vibrant lime margarita

TYPODARIUM

MAY

10

Saturday

LETRAFLEX

Letraflex, Display, 2024,
Art Grootfontein, www.grootfontein.net

Typography

ETHOLOGISTS

Water **FR**

SYNTA

TYPODARIUM

MAY

11

SUNDAY

TYPODARIUM

ABCDEFGH
IJKLMNOPQ
RSTUVWXYZ
0123456789

→ ↑ ←

Bixa, Display, 2015,
Mark van Wagningen, Novo Typo, www.novotypo.nl

BIXA

May

12

Wesak Day (MY)

Monday

Opera ABC

Opera ABC, Display, 2024,
Marinus Klinksik, www.marinusklinksik.de

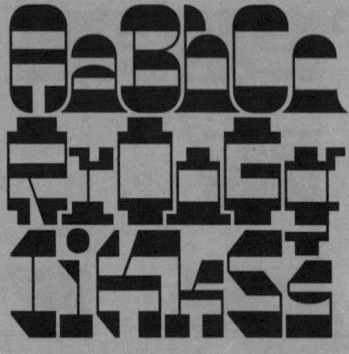

TYPODARIUM

May

13

Tuesday

Quark

Quark, Serif, 2023,
Mario De Libero, www.zetafonts.com

Electromagnetism
fundamental
Gravitation
constituents
Atomic Particle

TYPODARIUM

May

14

Wednesday

BohoBreeze

BohoBreeze, Display, 2024,
Lea Marie Schulz, www.instagram.com/leeaams

ABC
DEFunGHIJKL
MNOvaLPQRetroST
UVWXYZ

TYPODARIUM

May

15

Thursday

Kyoshi

Kyoshi, Pixel, 2023,
Alanna Munro, www.alannamunro.com

TYPODARIUM

MAY

16

General Prayer Day (DK)

FRIDAY

A SURREAL DREAM IN THE MEXICAN JUNGLE
ON AN ALMOST WINDLESS DAY
THE FOUR CANDLES BURN STRAIGHT
IN THE FOREST
DREAMING AT NOON

James, Display, 2025,
Néstor Rocha, www.nestbranding.com

JAMES

MAY

17

Constitution Day (NO)

SATURDAY

PENNEQUIN

Pennequin, Display, 2024,
Jo De Baerdemaeker, www.studiotype.be

PENNEQUIN IS PART OF
THE TYPO BELGIQUE
PROJECT & REVIVES
A METAL TYPEFACE
FROM THE EARLY
NINETEENTH CENTURY.
THAT ORIGINATES FROM
THE BRUSSELS-BASED
TYPE FOUNDRY OF
CHARLES PENNEQUIN

TYPODARIUM

MAY

18

Battle of Las Piedras (UR)

SUNDAY

BRINCA

Brinca, Variable, 2023,
In-House, www.weareinhouse.com

JAGGED AND BOUNCY

TYPODARIUM

May

19

Victoria Day (CA), Atatürk Commemoration and Youth Day (TR)

Monday

Basilar

Basilar, Sans, 2023,
Rui Abreu, www.r-typography.com

Sealing cover patch **thigh cable guide**

TYPODARIUM

May

20

Tuesday

Non Ophelie Display

Non Ophelie Display, Display, 2024,
Jona Saucedo, www.nonfoundry.com

The
Ophelias
Neil Young
on High
fft. Julien
Baker

~

TYPODARIUM

May

21

Navy Day (CL)

Wednesday

Snaga Grotesk

Snaga Grotesk, Sans, 2024,
Botio Nikoltchev & Trifon Andreev, www.lettersoup.de

Fotogravurzeichner

шрифтова култура

Schriftmetall

две схожие технологии

γραφικό σχέδιο

TYPODARIUM

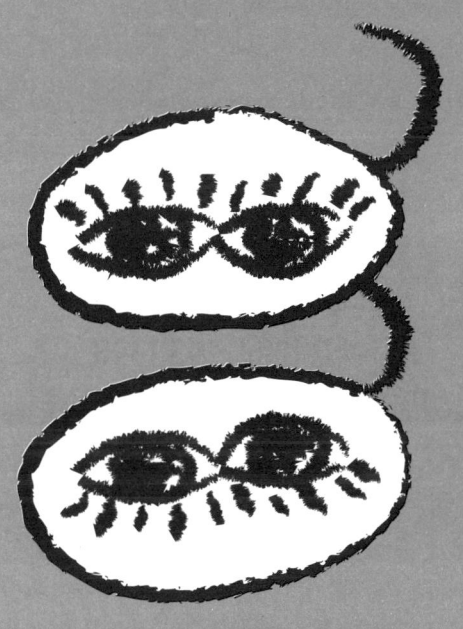

G like Gemini
21 May - 21 June

Zodiac Alphabet

Zodiac Alphabet, Typo-Illustration, 2024,
Manuel Viergutz, www.TypoGraphicDesign.de

Manuel Viergutz is a
Graphic-Designer,
Type-Designer &
Lettering-Artist based
in Berlin. Founder of
the Font-Foundry
TypoGraphicDesign.de

TYPODARIUM

May

22

Thursday

Alestalgia

Alestalgia, Serif, 2024,
Víctor Gómez, www.laletreria.co

There's **no** *pure* emōtion, *they* all̦ ***mutate*** in **oŭr** bødieš & **souɫs.**

* * * * * *

Alegría + *Nostalgia* = *Ales***talgia**

TYPODARIUM

May

23

Friday

Adelbrook

Adelbrook, Variable Serif, 2021,
Philip Lammert, www.vibrant-types.com

Kind of Leaning Verticals

Asymmetrical Idiosyncrasies

Firmly Rooted Characters

Harmonious Brush Pattern

Maintaining Quiet Zen

Established Upward Nature

Dynamic Serif Typeface

Obvious Weighty Gravity

TYPODARIUM

May

24

Bulgarian Education and Culture,
and Slavonic Literature Day (BG)

Saturday

Wesna

Wesna, Sans, 2022,
Alja Herlah, www.type-salon.com

Sharp Objects

functional type

Unique Cat Names

Condensed Answer

Yugo posters

morning koffe

TYPODARIUM

MAY

May Revolution Day (AR)

MISTO FONT

Misto Font, Display, 2019,
Kateryna Korolevtseva, www.korolevtseva.com

BRAVERY

COURAGE

UKRAINE

FREEDOM

STRENGTH

May

26

Spring Bank Holiday (GB), Memorial Day (USA)

Monday

Arrieta

Arrieta, Serif, 2023,
Diego Aravena Silo, www.wtypefoundry.com

ARRIETA WAS MADE BY A LAZY PUNCHCUTTER

The lazy punchcutter would cut letters with fewer curves, but still maintain a similar tone to OLD STYLES when used in small sizes.

TYPODARIUM

May

27

Mother's Day (BO)

TUESDAY

Postea

Postea, Sans, 2023, A. Alameddine, V. Burian, V. Evstañeva,
T. Grace, J. Scaglione, www.type-together.com/postea-multiscript

TYPODARIUM

may

28

Wednesday

FOR LARGE HEADLINES
AND EXPRESSIVE TYPOGRAPHY,
FOUR WEIGHTS.

Velvet XX Condenced Grotesk, Sans, 2024,
Michael Chereda, www.behance.net/brightheadstudio

VELVET XX CONDENCED GROTESK

May

Ascension Day

THURSDAY

SIXTEN

Sixten, Display, 2023,
Noel Pretorius, María Ramos, www.nmtype.com

SIXTEN IS A NEW TYPEFACE INSPIRED BY A CHILD'S LIMITLESS WAY OF APPROACHING LETTERSHAPES

5 WEIGHTS

3 WIDTHS

TYPODARIUM

May

30

Friday

HD Sans

HD Sans, Sans, 2024,
Mathew Prada, www.bastardatype.com/fonts

This typeface is a response to the abundant Neogrotesque font supply.

Although it is a Sans serif family, it offers a visually less common alternative, proposing a *medium contrast geometric style.*

12 styles: 6 weights, Regular→Heavy + slanted + 75 dingbats

✿☝☺☻♡♋⌂♠♞Q✄✂☉◠⊙◐◑⊕⊗△⌐⌙⊏⊐⌑▭⛶♍↺◡✓✗↗↦➡

∏∏∏∏∏∏∏∏∏∏∏∏

TYPODARIUM

MAY

31

Dragon Boat Festival (CN),
Tet Doan Ngo (Mid-Year Festival) (VN)

SATURDAY

Jaini

Jaini, Display, 2023,
Taresh Vohra, Ek Type, www.ektype.in

tejōvṛṣō dyutidharaḥ sarvaśastrabhṛtāṁ varaḥ |
pragrahō nigrahō vyagrō naikaśṛṅgō gadāgrajaḥ || 81 ||

caturmūrtiścaturbāhuścaturvyūhaścaturgatiḥ |
caturātmā caturbhāvaścaturvedavidekapāt || 82 ||

samāvartō nivṛttātmā durjayō duratikramaḥ |
durlabhō durgamō durgō durāvāsō durārihā || 83 ||

śubhāṅgō lōkasāraṅgaḥ sutantustantuvardhanaḥ |
indrakarmā mahākarmā kṛtakarmā kṛtāgamaḥ || 84 ||

TYPODARIUM

june

1

Children's Day (RO)

sunday

flowering

arkansas

norwich

ascended

Penelope, Variable Unicase Display, 2024.
Jacob Wise, www.wisetype.nl

Penelope

JUNE

2

Republic Day (IT), King's Birthday (MY)

MONDAY

Arch, Display, 2024,
Katharina Valkenkamp, www.kava-kreativ.de

arch

JUNE

3

Tuesday

LDN KINGS ROAD

LDN Kings Road. Display. 2024.
Paul Harpin. www.londontype.co.uk

KINGS **ROAD**
KINGS **ROAD**
KINGS ROAD
KINGS ROAD

TYPODARIUM

JUNE

4

WEDNESDAY

VTG STENCIL DIAG-B 087

Vtg Stencil Diag-B 087, Stencil, 2023,
Andreas Seidel, www.astype.de, fontstore.astype.com

A TRADITIONAL STENCIL TYPEFACE FOR MARKING.

DESIGNED FROM AN 0.875 INCH DIAGRAPH-BRADLEY STENCIL CUTTING MACHINE.

TYPODARIUM

JUNE

5

Constitution Day (DK)

THURSDAY

CAPTOON

Captoon. Display, 2023.
Antia Jürgeleit, www.typethis.studio

KETCHUP
IS TECHNICALLY A
FRUIT
SMOOTHIE
HAPPY KETCHUP DAY (US)

TYPODARIUM

June

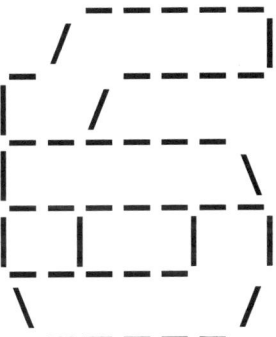

6

Memorial Day (KR), Swedish National Day (SE),
Eid al-Adha (ID, LB), Hari Raya Haji (MY)

Friday

BD Asciimax, Display, 1999/2023,
Lopetz, Büro Destruct, www.typedifferent.com

June

Saturday

Austerlitz

Austerlitz, Serif, 2022,
Jean François Porchez, www.typofonderie.com

10th December 1948

FREEDOM OF THOUGHT

Constitution

Collective consciousness

EQUALITY

TYPODARIUM

June

8

Pentecost (Whit Sunday) (DK, PL)

Sunday

Glycerin

Glycerin, Variable Sans, 2023,
Roch Modrzejewski, www.rohhtype.com

Shape-shifting

arts & joy

Glycerin is a contemporary geo-humanist sans serif variable type family offering excellent legibility and strong personality It is designed to be used for paragraph text, **while its heavy variants create unique and powerful display scenarios.**

TYPODARIUM

JUNE

9

Kings Birthday (AU), Pentecost day

MONDAY

CYCLOPS

Cyclops, Display, 2023,
Hannes von Döhren, www.hvdfonts.com

STRONG LIKE CYCLOPS

TYPODARIUM

JUNE

10

Portugal Day (PT)

Tuesday

GeoMD

GeoMD, Display, Sans, Text, 2012,
Márcio Duarte, www.peji.com.br

A typography based on geometric right angles by its simplicity of form and orderly appearance.

TYPODARIUM

JUNE

II

WEDNESDAY

POMPEJI23

POMPEJI23, Serif, 2023,
makes no semse, www.no-semse.com

ABCDEFG
HIJKLM&...
† : INSPIRED BY THE
GRAFITTI FROM * !
POMPEII // GI GE U

TYPODARIUM

JUNE

12

Russia Day (Unity Day) (RU)

THURSDAY

APK BUITENWIJK

APK Buitenwijk, Display, 2024,
Autograph Peter Korsman, www.apk-type.com

B-W/RSM
2024®

TYPODARIUM

JUNE

13

Friday

Easy Grotesk

Easy Grotesk, Variable Sans, 2023,
Olivia Wood & Alexander Rütten, www.TypeMates.com

Relax!

It's Fiday the 13th. SO WHAT?!

→ This ultra friendly typeface originally designed for a tech startup, its seven styles, *matching italics* and relaxed attitude can organise complex information and make it approachable. Easy.

TYPODARIUM

June

14

Saturday

LeOsler

Leosler, Display, 2015,
Julia Martinez Diana, www.antipixel.com.ar

☀ **SCRAPBOOKING** ✳

(graphic photo diary)

handcrafted

〰 sketch & collage 〰

TYPODARIUM

JUNE

15

SUNDAY

SWONO

Swono, Mono Grotesque, 2023,
Fabian Dornhecker, www.laboldevita.com

ABIOGENICALLY
NAPHTHALISING
FJÖLÞJÓÐLEGUR
XEROPHTHALMIA
ZWERGWACHTELN
PSIQUIÁTRICOS
ULTRAFAMILIAR
ZINCOGRAPHERS
TOLSTOISERENT

TYPODARIUM

June

16

Monday

F37 Sonic

F37 Sonic, Sans, 2023,
F37 Foundry, www.f37foundry.com

An unusual geometric sans serif that amplifies your messages. Sharp, striking and impactful, it calls out for attention.

Light *Italic* Regular *Italic* Medium *Italic* **Bold** *Italic*
Extra Bold *Italic* **Black** *Italic* **Ultra Black** *Italic*
0123456789 .,:" ([{!?@£$%&}])

TYPODARIUM

June

17

Tuesday

Sandhouse

Sandhouse, Display, 2023,
Sandra Garcia, Tipastype, www.ilovetypography.com

call me#

POP FEST

Cool&Soft

Tons of joy

it's my party!

0123456789

TYPODARIUM

 JUNE

18

 Wednesday

HEADLINE Poster

Headline Poster, Variable Sans, 2023,
Manuel Viergutz, www.TypoGraphicDesign.de

TYPODARIUM

June

19

Corpus Christi (CO)

Thursday

华光字库 新宋

HuaguangXinsong, Display, 2023,
Xing Zhichao/Song Yingming, www.hgfonts.com

三十功名尘与土八
千里路云和月莫等
闲白了少年头空悲
切此岳武穆满江红
词句也作者自六岁
时即口受记忆至今
喜诵之不衰自今以
往弃哀时客之名更
自名曰少年中国之

少年

TYPODARIUM

JUNE

20

National Flag Day (AR)

Friday

Supertall, Display Sans, 2023,
Adam Greasley, www.colttypeco.com

MAKING STATEMENTS

Regular
Bold
Oblique
Boblique

TYPODARIUM

JUNE

21

Midsummer's Day (SE)

SATURDAY

TYPODARIUM

KIT CROWD: Dingbat & Display, 2024,
Kwangmoo Lee & Heejae Yang, www.ktowntype.com

C like Cancer
22 June - 22 July

Zodiac Alphabet

Zodiac Alphabet, Typo-Illustration, 2024,
Manuel Viergutz, www.TypoGraphicDesign.de

Manuel Viergutz is a
Graphic-Designer,
Type-Designer &
Lettering-Artist based
in Berlin. Founder of
the Font-Foundry
TypoGraphicDesign.de

June

22

Sunday

Galante Mono

Galante Mono, Display, 2025.
Maël Bächtold, www.maelbachtold.ch

junkyards

EQUIVOCAL

kingcraft

BLINDSPOT

TYPODARIUM

JUNE

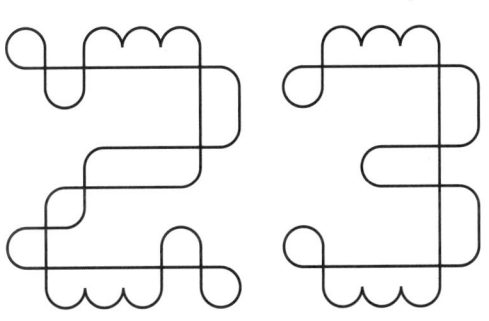

23

Victory Day (EE)

MONDAY

Figure 8. Display, 2023,
Paul Bokslag, www.paulbokslag.com

JUNE

24

Midsummer Day (EE)

TUESDAY

Kablammo, Variable Display, 2023,
Vectro, www.vectrotype.com

KABLAMMO

June

25

Statehood Day (SI)

Wednesday

Artusi

Artusi, Serif, 2022,
Francesco Canovaro, www.zetafonts.com

¾ Teaspoon

napoli's pizza

Journey

carbonara

TYPODARIUM

June

26

Islamic New Year (ID, LB)

Thursday

Latin Multilingual

Delicate Honeymooners

Summer season's fashion trends 2025

Early Modernist

Orchestrale

Operetta Italics, Display Serif, 2023,
Jan Tonellato, https://typography.synthview.com

Operetta Italics

June

27

Friday

Dynamis

Dynamis, Variable, 2024,
Lucas Guizetti, www.lucasguizetti.cargo.site

A diverse variable font, full of Pride!

{Stonewall} ß **QUEER**

Visibility *1969–2025

🌈 **Empôwering** » z

stéreotÿpe; Rešilience

ABCDEFGHIJKLMNOPQRSTUVWXYZ 0123456789
abcdefghijklmnopqrstuvwxyz .,:;!?@$€§%+−×÷=

TYPODARIUM

June

28

Saturday

Nora-Note

Nora-Note. Script, 2024,
Elena Schönsee, www.elena-schoensee.de

Dear Dairy
I will take over
the world today.

xoxo

TYPODARIUM

JUNE

29

Saint Peter and Saint Paul (CL)

Sunday

OT 2049

OT 2049, Mono, 2024, Fred Wiltshire,
Mat Desjardins, Francesca Bolognini, www.off-type.com

VOIGHT-KAMPFF
Tyrell CORP
BATTY (Roy)
NEXUS VI
Combat Model

TYPODARIUM

June

30

Sacred Heart (CO)

Monday

Diligence

Diligence, Text & Display, 2024,
Paul Hanslow with Kaja Słojewska, www.tandemtype.co

FABRIQUE de CHAPEAUX

Charleston speakeasy

Théâtre des Champs-Élysées

1920–1934

Putting on the Ritz

"Oh, that Transatlantic Accent"

Prohibition-era Ragamuffin!

TYPODARIUM

July

1

Canada Day (CA)

Tuesday

RR·Trivium

RR-Trivium, Display, 2025,
Rafeal Ramirez Lozano, BajioType, www.bajiotype.com

Stopwars

A ÁB C D E E F G H II
J K L L M N Ñ N O Ó Ö
R S T U Ú Ü W X Y Z
a á b c d e é f g h i j k l m
n o ó ö p q r s t u ú ü w x y z
1 2 3 4 5 6 7 8 9 0

TYPODARIUM

JULY

2

WEDNESDAY

TT Ricordi Greto

TT Ricordi Greto, Sans, 2021,
TypeType Foundry, www.typetype.org

DYING TO LIVE

TYPODARIUM

JULY

3

THURSDAY

BEE FONT

Bee Font, Sans, 2023,
Manuel Viergutz & G, www.TypoGraphicDesign.de

TYPODARIUM

JULY

04

Independence Day (USA)

FRIDAY

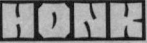

Honk, Display Variable Colour, 2023,
Yesha Goshar & Noopur Datye, ektype.in/honk

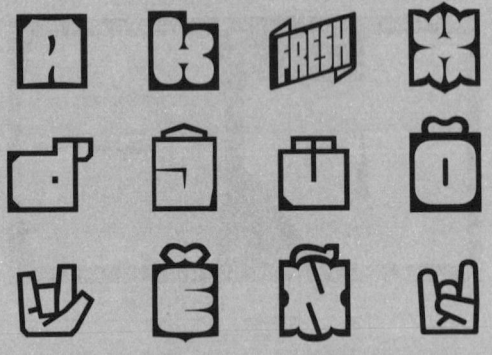

TYPODARIUM

July

5

Saints Cyril and Methodius Day (CZ)

Saturday

Everett Pan

Everett Pan, Sans, 2024,
Nolan Paparelli, www.nolan-paparelli.ch

Θα ζυγίσω
χίλια εξακόσια
εβδομήντα πέντε
φρέσκα ψωμιά

TYPODARIUM

July

6

Jan Hus Day (CZ)

Sunday

Perva

Perva, Display, 2021,
Emerson Eller, www.ellertype.com

Slab

Reverse

Black

A family of three eye-catching fonts

TYPODARIUM

July

7

Monday

Moucha

Moucha, Variable Sans, 2023,
Philip Lammert, www.vibrant-types.com

Large Eelgrass Filtering 498 ₦

Large Eelgrass Filtering 498 ₦

★☆ Intertidal Mudflats Kelp?

★☆ Intertidal Mudflats Kelp?

Blue-Green Algae Risk ☞

Blue-Green Algae Risk ☞

TYPODARIUM

Juli

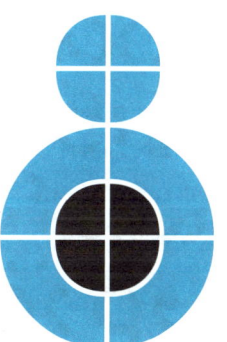

Tuesday

vwxyz
opqrstu
hijklmn
abcdefg

Ole, Display, 2025,
Lisa Dröes, Lisadroes.nl

Ole

JULY

9

Independence Day (AR)

Wednesday

PLAYPEN SANS

Playpen Sans, Sans, 2023, Veronika Burian, Laura Meseguer,
José Scaglione, www.type-together.com/playpen-sans-font

Digital
Avocado
Superhero
Typography
Empequeñecer
Taramasalata

July

10

Thursday

Guust

Guust, Display Sans, 2024,
Jo De Baerdemaeker, www.studiotype.be

Guust: this unique display typeface for editorial & poster design is inspired by a printing type of Fonderie Typographique A. Vanderborght & Dumont, a Belgian type foundry that operated from Brussels in the 19th and 20th century.

Guust is part of 'Typo Belgiëque', a design & research project that breathes new life into Belgium's historical typeface families.

TYPODARIUM

July

11

Friday

Minorca

Minorca, Serif, 2024,
Solenn Bordeau, www.black-foundry.com

Hooky Display Type

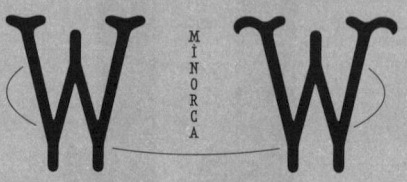

The design of the hook allows traction forces to be relayed through
the curved portion to and from the proximal end of the hook.

TYPODARIUM

July

12

Saturday

PHONT

Phont, Sans, 2024,
Frederik Merkel & Katharina Gresch, www.phont.ai

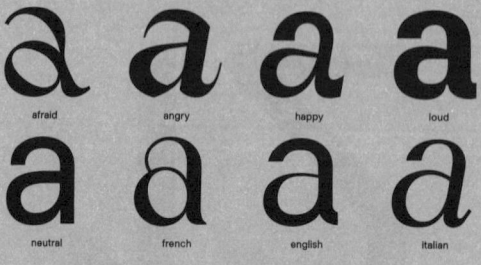

Using AI, Phont recognizes characteristics in spoken language and displays them with synaesthetic type design. We create subtitles as diverse as language itself.

TYPODARIUM

JULY

10

SUNDAY

PATA SLAB

Pata Slab, Display, 2021,
In-House, www.weareinhouse.com

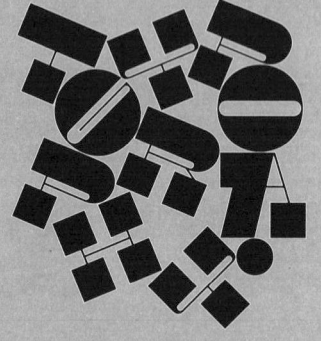

TYPODARIUM

JULY

14

Bastille Day (FR)

MONDAY

It's time to take a *Quick break*

Flaneur, Serif, 2023,
Frederick Wiltshire, fredsfonts.com

FLANEUR

JULY

15

Democracy and National Unity Day (TR)

TUESDAY

Plage Sans

Plage Sans, Sans, 2024,
Bouk Ra, www.bouk.work

Café Noir Dans Un Carré Noir

TYPODARIUM

July

16

Wednesday

Ferryman

Ferryman, Blackletter, 2023,
Felix Braden, www.floodfonts.com

Echo Chamber

85% Dark Matter

earth@univer.se

Lost Hangar 18

TYPODARIUM

July

17

Thursday

ROSSO

Rosso, Sans, 2022,
Gaspar Muñoz, www.wtypefoundry.com

ROSSO NORMAL & ALT

ROSLYN GOTHIC — Ultra Light
The Grand Prix — Light
Philip K. Dick — Regular
Metropolis — Bold
OPERATION — Black

TYPODARIUM

July

18

Constitution Day (UR)

Friday

WBP Emperio

WBP Emperio, Display, 2022,
Jasper Nijssen, www.jaspernijssen.nl

TYPODARIUM

july

saturday

Circoli

Circoli, Sans, 2023,
Maja Rüffer, www.instagram.com/major0609

Imagine walking on the beach:
toes caressing the sand grains.
Kids playing with a ball and
an old couple embracing each other.
While watching how the sun sets
and the moon rises.
- thats the circle of life -

TYPODARIUM

JULY

20

Independence Day (CO)

Sunday

Experimo™

Experimo™, Sans, 2024,
Tana Kosiyabong, www.r9typedesign.com

→ 6 WEIGHTS | 1,300+ GLYPHS EACH ←

0. Zéro   5. Fünf
1. Uno   6. Şase
2. Två   7. Седем
3. Três   8. Eight
4. Четыре 9. Nouă

↑ ↑ ↑ ↑ Experimo™ Medium at 16 pt ↑ ↑ ↑ ↑

TYPODARIUM

Юли   July

21

Belgian National Day (BE), Marine Day (JP)

Понеделник **Monday**

29LT Azahar LC Text & Display

29LT Azahar LC, Variable Serif, Display and Text Type, 2024,
José Carratala [Latin] & Krista Radoeva [Cyrillic], www.29LT.com

Hamburgefonts

Киберносуфа

Hamburgefonts

Киберносуфа

TYPODARIUM

JULY

22

TUESDAY

HOUSE BERLIN

House Berlin, Display, 2023,
Raban Ruddigkeit, www.ruddigkeit.de

ABCDEFG
HIJKLMN
OPQRSTU
VWXYZ

TYPODARIUM

L like Leo
23 July - 23 August

Zodiac Alphabet

Zodiac Alphabet, Typo-Illustration, 2024,
Manuel Viergutz, www.TypoGraphicDesign.de

Manuel Viergutz is a
Graphic-Designer,
Type-Designer &
Lettering-Artist based
in Berlin. Founder of
the Font-Foundry
TypoGraphicDesign.de

TYPODARIUM

July

23

Wednesday

Timezone Mono

HAL Timezone Mono, Serif, 2023,
HAL Typefaces, type.hanli.eu

Pacific Standard
Amazon Summer
Australian Central
South Vietnam
Eastern European
Mauritius GMT+4

July

24

Thursday

Foundry Tiento

Foundry Tiento, Display, 2020,
David Quay, Stuart de Rozario, www.thefoundrytypes.com

Neo-Classic *Modern*

Gracefully *Refined*

Subtly *Curvaceous*

Expressively *Fluid*

← ↑ → ↓ ↖ ↗ ↘ ↙

TYPODARIUM

JULY

25

FRIDAY

PROTEIN
BIOHANFÖL
DOPPEL
CBD-NÜSSE

Doppel, Display, 2023,
Jörg Walter, www.groupe-dejour.de

DOPPEL

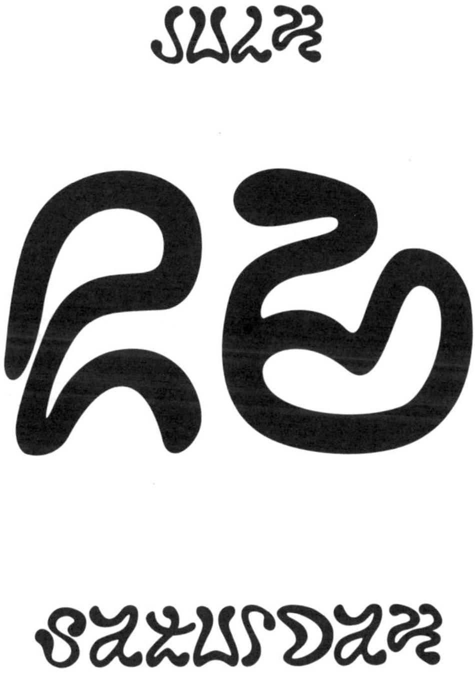

FLUID

Fluid, Display, 2023,
Yarza Twins, www.yarzatwins.com

HÖTEL
AUX
PIGEONS

TYPODARIUM

JULY

27

SUNDAY

BLAKE DISPLAY

Blake Display, Display, 2024,
Barrett Reid-Maroney, www.barrettrm.com

Bold

Regular

Light

TYPODARIUM

July

28

Monday

Macan Mono

Macan Mono, Mono, 2024,
Tightype, www.tightype.com

Mixmag

Frontpage

XLR8R

Raveline

De:Bug

TYPODARIUM

July

29

Tuesday

Leopardo

Leopardo, Display, 2023,
Alexandre Bassi, www.205.tf

Forest
Antelope
Roar
Yellowish

TYPODARIUM

JULY

30

Wednesday

OMNIUM

Omnium, Sans, 2019,
Robby Woodard, www.garagefonts.com

Conceptualisation

PROPELS SYSTEMATIZATION

Ascending Martially

Dehydrogenated

MIDI COUNTERBALANCES

Reindustrialization

TYPODARIUM

JULY

31

THURSDAY

FESTO

Festo, Script, 2013, Ewen Prigent,
www.myfonts.com/collection/festo-font-la-boite-graphique

REGATO IS A HAND MADE FONT IDEAL FOR YOUR GRAPHIC PROJECT. USAGE RECOMMENDATIONS : TITLE, SHORT TEXT, CHILDREN'S BOOK, POSTER, BOOK COVER, BROCHURE, LABEL, MAGAZINE

TYPODARIUM

AUGUST

Swiss National Day (CH)

FRIDAY

EGGCELLENT

Eggcellent, Display, 2023,
Julia Hell, www.julia-hell.com

JOYFUL HENS
LAY EXQUISITE EGGS
WITH WARMTH
AND CARE

TYPODARIUM

AUGUST

TWO

SATURDAY

DRAGO

DRAGO, Display, 2024,
Tomasz Pawluk, instagram.com/bosfff

TYPODARIUM

August

Sunday

KEYFRAME

Keyframe, Display, 2023,
Lucas Descroix, www.plain-form.com

Biodiversity of the CONCRETE ISLANDS: a Guide

TYPODARIUM

August

Monday

Aquawax **Fx**

Aquawax Fx, Sans, 2022,
Francesco Canovaro & Mario De Libero, www.zetafonts.com

The Way of Water

chemical formula

Υδροσφαίρα

INKTRAPS

science fiction

TYPODARIUM

August

5

Tuesday

Vitamiin

Vitamiin, Variable Sans, 2024.
Andree Paat, www.typokompanii.com

Dreamy Indie & Bedroom Pop

AUGUST

6

Independence Day (BO)

WEDNESDAY

KREIS

KREIS, Display, 2022,
Kateryna Korolevtseva, www.korolevtseva.com.

THE TRUTH DOESN'T DROWN IN WATER & DOESN'T BURN IN FIRE

August

7

Thursday

Brel

Brel, Display Text Serif, 2024,
Jo De Baerdemaeker, www.studiotype.be

Brel is a unique typeface that originates from the type collection of A. Vanderborght & Dumont, a 19th century Belgian type foundry in Brussels.

Brel is part of 'Typo Belgiëque', a design & research project that breathes new life into Belgium's historical typeface families.

TYPODARIUM

August

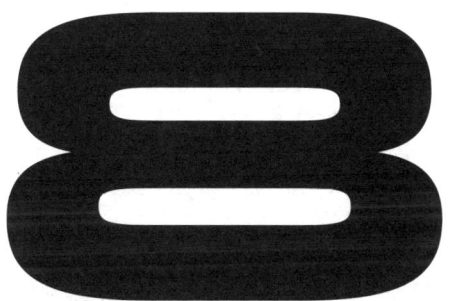

Friday

YFF RARE

YFF Rare, Variable Sans, 2023,
www.paratype.com/fonts/yff/yff-rare

RR

Arrows↑↔↟↠↡·**Bullits**▶▷◆◇

Coins ①②③④⑤⑥⑦⑧⑨⓪⓿

From extra condensed **to hyper**

WIDE

❶❷❸❹❺❻❼❽❾⊕✪

TYPODARIUM

August

Saturday

Rethink

Rethink, Sans, 2023,
Viktor Nübel, www.viktornuebel.com

To draw attention to important and relevant topics is not only a question of using the right words, but also the right tone. For written messages it needs the support of *a strong and unique typographic voice!*
Take the time needed, rethink and choose your type carefully.

TYPODARIUM

AUGUST

10

SUNDAY

RIG SOLID

Rig Solid, Display, 2018.
Jamie Clarke, www.jamieclarketype.com.

EXPANSIONARY
REINVENTIONS
TERRAFORMED
INFILTRATIONS
QUESTIONINGS

TYPODARIUM

AUGUST

11

Mountain Day (JP)

Monday

VZWO Choreo

VZWO Choreo, Display & Text, 2023,
Viktor Zumegen, www.viktorzumegen.de

Display Thin Italic

Display Black Italic

□ Text Regular ◇ *Italic*

■ ◆

TYPODARIUM

August

12

TUESDAY

Gimpel

Gimpel, Variable Sans, 2023,
David Henni Wiesner, www.davidwiesner.de

düüh

Single-minded like a swarm — free like a BIRD.

TYPODARIUM

August

13

Wednesday

OTC Oituz

OTC Oituz, Sans, 2024,
Ograda Type Company, www.ograda.co

Another fact to bear in mind is that
a good deal of this knowledge just
cannot be stated verbally. That
everything can be made clear through
words is a very short-sighted and
perhaps recent idea. Thus, when
the pupil has reached a certain
level of experience, the master will
not explain, but literally show him

TYPODARIUM

August

Thursday

Swizzy

Swizzy, Sans, 2023,
Jan Weidemüller, www.ultra-kuhl.com

AB€Đ↓↑123@®åbc™

TYPODARIUM

August

15

Assumption of Mary, Independence Day (IN),
Liberation Day (KR)

Friday

Volut

Volut, Display, 2023,
Christoph Ulherr, www.jpfonts.com

Låţïŋ Pŕø
4 design variations
→ charming characters
& funky features,
e.g. a co fl Th st ...
Boom!

TYPODARIUM

August

16

Saturday

NaR Partition

NaR Partition, Display Italic, 2025
Đông Trúc, https://www.instagram.com/do_ngtruc/

NaR stands for Not-a-Revival

TYPODARIUM

AUGUST

17

Independence Day (ID), San Martín Day (AR)

SUNDAY

SKEWY

Skewy, Display, 2023.
Andre Toet, www.andretoet.com

DO NOT SEEK PRAISE, SEEK CRITICISM !

Paul Arden

TYPODARIUM

August

18

Monday

Scotch Roman

Scotch Roman, Serif, 2024,
Trifon Andreev, www.trifonandreev.com

Ein Gegenvorschlag

съвременен шрифт

Buchdruckerkunst

хуманистичен

Cyrillic convention

August

19

Tuesday

BD Orange

BD Orange, Variable Sans, 2023,
Lopetz, Büro Destruct, www.typediffer/net.com

featuring more than 1'021 Glyphs in **5** Weights from delicate Thin to **Loud Black** and a Fruit-Basket full of **Alternatives**, Discretionary Ligatures →UPPERCASE— Greek + Cyrillic & JAPANESE Katakana. スパークリング*

TYPODARIUM

August ☀

20

Restoration of Independence Day (EE)

 Wednesday

Diglû

Diglû. Sans. 2019.
Emphase. www.diglu.ch

Transform your 💬 words
into a 🐦 visual journey
with Diglû, featuring
over 1500 pictograms 🦖
👁🖱 available in ten
🎚 weights, from hairline
to black ⊘ 👏 📢.

TYPODARIUM

August

21

Thursday

CA Spotnik Serif

CA Spontik Serif. Serif, 2024.
Stefan Claudius. www.cape-arcona.com

»NASA's Latest
Space Mission Sends
Rover to Explore
Uncharted Terrain
on Mars«

$01234 ↔ 56789€

TYPODARIUM

August

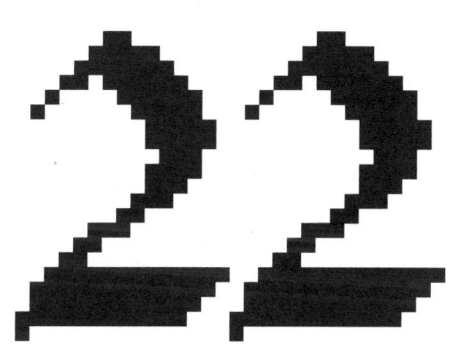

22

Friday

Pixelcastle

Pixelcastle, Display, 2023,
Leonhard Katschner, www.bravetype.de

Sphinx of
black quartz
judge my vow.

TYPODARIUM

August

23

Saturday

Axalp Grotesk

Axalp Grotesk, Variable Sans, 2022,
Roch Modrzejewski, www.rohhtype.com

Axalp Grotesk is a modernist sans
serif type family characterized by
the play between elegant rounded
shapes and sharp angular details.

It is bright, crisp and charismatic, being an
attractive contemporary alternative to the
popular classics of Swiss design school.

Stadtcasino Basel

TYPODARIUM

V like Virgo
24 August - 23 September

Zodiac Alphabet

Zodiac Alphabet, Typo-Illustration, 2024,
Manuel Viergutz, www.TypoGraphicDesign.de

Manuel Viergutz is a
Graphic-Designer,
Type-Designer &
Lettering-Artist based
in Berlin. Founder of
the Font-Foundry
TypoGraphicDesign.de

TYPODARIUM

August

24

Sunday

Waverse

Waverse, Display, 2023.
Tien Min Liao, www.typeji.com

ABCDEFGHIJKLMNOPQRSTUVWXYZ
abcdefghijklmnopqrstuvwxyz@!?
$£€¥₩₤₽{&}§©®™%‰0123456789
☺☹☻✦✚♠☒☑♫♥←↑→↓↔↕(§)[¼½¾].,!?

August

25

Summer Bank Holiday (GB), Independence Day (UR)

Monday

Banana Milk

Banana Milk, Display, 2023.
Adam Greasley, www.colttypeco.com

Glug, Glug, Glug... Aahhhh

TYPODARIUM

AUGUST

TUESDAY

Fart, Display, 2024.
Li Zhiqian, www.jtype.cn

FART

August

27

Wednesday

slack

Slack, Display, 2024.
Jozef Ondrik, Matej Vojtuš, www.regularlines.com

AaBbCcDd
EeFfGgHhIi
JjKkLlMmNn
OoPpQqRrSs
TtUuVvWwLLuu
XxYyZz->%‰↑↓

TYPODARIUM

August

28

Thursday

Skrappa

Skrappa, Variable, 2024,
Jacob Wise, www.wisetype.nl

Märklin™ Trains
Banal Corporate Messaging
Transportation
Great Hovercraft Facilities
Black & Decker

TYPODARIUM

August

29

Friday

Stacja Europa

Stacja Europa, Stencil, 2024,
Roman Wilhelm, www.romantype.net.

Przystanek autobusowy
Peron 12 Kołobrzeg, Mielno
Proszę czekać 14:45
Do Warszawy; do Szczecina
Reduta Morast 1853

TYPODARIUM

August

30

Victory Day (TR)

Saturday

Algorytm

Algorytm, Sans, 2024,
Interval Type, www.intervaltype.com

Algorytm Norm

Algorytm Office

Algorytm Flip

Algorytm Mono

Algorytm Soft

Algorytm Sport

TYPODARIUM

august

31

sunday

dina Chaumont

Dina Chaumont, Display Mono, 2023, André Baldinger,
Toan Vu-Huu, Jimmy Le Guennec, Fanny Hamelin, www.bvhtype.com

Light regular bold

extra bold black

TYPODARIUM

September

1

Labour Day (CA, USA)

Monday

Geometrico *Slab*

Geometrico Slab, Slab, 2023,
Filippo Salmina, www.geometrico.ch

Should it express power?
Geometric and Slabserifs: a
relatively rare combination.
Geometrico Slab takes its cue
from Herb Lubalin's typeface
family of the same name, and by
using optical corrections with
restraint, it looks a touch more
uncompromising. **Curious?** Try
Geometrico Slab free of charge.

TYPODARIUM

September

2

National Day (VN)

Tuesday

Velos Mono

Velos Mono, Serif, 2023,
Christian Gruber, www.scifipoetry.de

Sphinx \ of °
*, [−] black
« quartz • × ¶
judge…my † ¬
» ©^ _ ! vow#?

TYPODARIUM

September

Wednesday

Non Bureau Extended

Non Bureau Extended, Sans, 2023,
Jona Saucedo, www.nonfoundry.com

(Andy Sttot)
ΠροβλήματαLuxury
πολυτέλειας
ProblemsΜοντέρνα
Modern
ΑγπηLove

TYPODARIUM

September

4

Thursday

Chaparrita

Chaparrita, Script, 2023,
Dafne Martinez, Tipastype, www.ilovetypography.com

If I'm shining, everybody gonna shine!

Chaparrita
(a yummi dancing font)

❁

TYPODARIUM

september

5

FRIDAY

snaga unicase

Snaga Unicase, Sans, 2024,
Botio Nikoltchev & Trifon Adreev, www.lettersoup.com

ROUND & SQUARED

MAJUSCULE

conventions

ОВАЛЕН И ЪГЛЕСТ

МАЮСКУЛ

TYPODARIUM

SEPTEMBER

Unification Day (BG)

Saturday

Cymbal

Cymbal, Sans, 2025,
Linus Knappe, www.nicetotype.jp

Attention! (Zombie)
Quick march (Zombie)
Slow march (Zombie)
Left turn (Zombie)
Right turn (Zombie)
About turn (Zombie)
Double up (Zombie)
Salute (Zombie)
Open your hat (Zombie)
Stand at ease (Zombie)
Fall in (Zombie)
Fall out (Zombie)
Fall down (Zombie)
Get ready! (Zombie)

Lyrics: Fela Kuti

TYPODARIUM

September

7

Independence Day (BR)

Sunday

Amnezia

Amnezia, Script, 2024,
Arthur Schwarz, www.productiontype.com

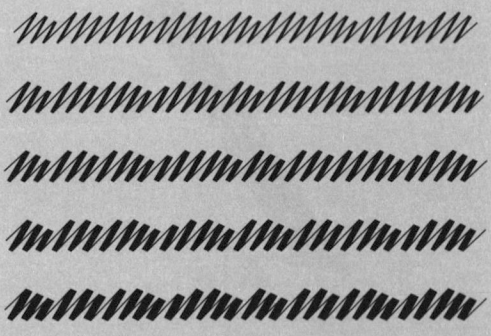

TYPODARIUM

September

8

Monday

Ostervald

Ostervald, Sans, 2024,
Maël Bächtold, www.maelbachtold.ch

1815*Neuchâtel
Bevaix & {MILVIGNES}
→ La Côte-aux-Fées ↓
LE CERNEUX-PEQUIGNOT
Rochefort † Cortaillod
«VAL-DE-TRAVERS» 62

TYPODARIUM

SEPTEMBER

TUESDAY

SEX MACHINE

Sex Machine, Display, 2023,
Mattia Luise, Ariel Brandolini, www.design-associati.it

TYPODARIUM

September

10

Wednesday

Foundry Arkias

Foundry Arkias, Display, 2023,
David Quay, Stuart de Rozario, www.thefoundrytypes.com

Harmonious Compositions

Arched Characteristics

Contemporarily Distinctive

Modular Interpretation

Multiple Alternatives

Distinguishable Axis

TYPODARIUM

September

11

Thursday

Paraiso Sans

Paraiso, Sans, 2022,
Lucas Descroix, www.plain-form.com

"Of radishes and generic maintenance"

TYPODARIUM

September

12

Friday

Balkenschrift

Balkenschrift, Variable Sans, 2024,
Gabriel Richter & Andreas Uebele, www.nicetotype.jp

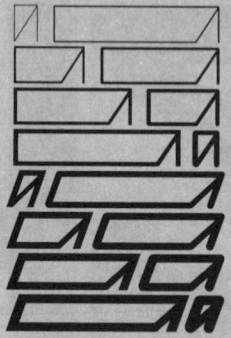

TYPODARIUM

September

13

Saturday

Taxa

Taxa, Sans, 2024,
Jong-Beom Kim, www.nodetonode.kr

Pachypodium gracilius

Ginkgo biloba

Dorstenia gigas

Canis lupus familiaris

Felis silvestris catus

TYPODARIUM

SEPTEMBER

FOURTEEN

SUNDAY

Malutzki Initials, Display, 2023,
Peter Malutzki, Lena Schmidt, www.spiritandbonesdesign.com

September

15

Respect for the Aged Day (JP)

Monday

GO Trax

GO Trax, Sans, 2024,
Samuel Götschin, www.samuelgoetsch.in

(Acid House)
Nachtschicht
Fader; 1998“
[Drum↔Bass]
45 rpm · 16Ø*

TYPODARIUM

September

16

Independence Day (MX), National Day (MY)

Tuesday

Bigante, Variable Sans, 2024,
Philip Lammert, www.vibrant-types.com

Bigante

September

17

Wednesday

Droulers Clarendon

Droulers Clarendon, Serif, 2024,
Bureau Brut, www.bureaubrut.com

Droulers Clarendon Line *Italic*
Droulers Clarendon Light *Italic*
Droulers Clarendon Book *Italic*
Droulers Clarendon Regular *Italic*
Droulers Clarendon Medium *Italic*
Droulers Clarendon Bold *Italic*
Droulers Clarendon Extrabold *Italic*
Droulers Clarendon Black *Italic*

TYPODARIUM

September

18

National Day (CL)

Thursday

Arsen

Arsen, Serif, 2023,
Joachim Vu, www.typofonderie.com

Philharmonic

Imagination doesn't stay cold

THEATRE

Place de l'Hôtel-de-Ville

Great classical

TYPODARIUM

TYPODARIUM
2025

OUT NOW!

TYPODARIUM

September

19

Day of the Glories of the Army (CL)

Friday

Barnum

Barnum, Serif, 2023,
Cosimo Lorenzo Pancini, www.zetafonts.com

Alessandro Baricco
contemporary
Rejuvenate
impactful
Novecento

TYPODARIUM

September

20

Saturday

Cy

Cy, Sans, 2018,
Prof. Jürgen Huber, supertype®, www.supertype.de/fonts/cy

AAAAaaaa BBBbb CCCCcc Ddd
EEeee Fff GGggg Hhh IIii JJJjj
KKkk Lll MMMΠmm NNΠnn
OΠoo PPpp QQqq RRrr SSss
Ttt UUuu VVvv WWwww XXxx
YYyyy ZZzz · 1122 3344 5б6
7788 9900 &&&& ?!#@¾]·}·)

9 Weights: Thin to Black

TYPODARIUM

SEPTEMBER

21

SUNDAY

GAWKER 2.0

Gawker 2.0, Display, 2023,
Tyler McFaul, www.tylermcfaul.design

← UMBRA →

‡ MESONIC ‡

* VAMOOSE *

• NEPOTISM •

↔ SYCAMORE ↕

" AMOEBOUS "

TYPODARIUM

September

22

Independence Day (BG)

Monday

Harmony in Fishwell

The Enchanted Garden, Script, 2023,
Gulya Yeap, www.peachcreme.com

The Enchanted Garden

September

23

Autumnal Equinox Day (JP)

Tuesday

Avona Serif

Avona Serif, Serif, 2021,
Alanna Munro, www.alannamunro.com

g Charisma
Intelligence
Dexterity
Constitution
Wisdom
Strength

TYPODARIUM

September

24

Wednesday

Timez

Timez, Serif, 2022,
Fabian Dorhecker, www.laboldevita.com

❧ Readable Timez Regular
Italic Book *Italic* Medium *Italic*
SemiBold *Italic* **Bold** *Italic*
❧ Casual Timez Regular
Italic Book *Italic* Medium *Italic*
SemiBold *Italic* **Bold** *Italic*
❧ Strange Timez Regular
Italic Book *Italic* Medium *Italic*
SemiBold *Italic* **Bold** *Italic*

L like Libra
24 September - 23 October

Zodiac Alphabet

Zodiac Alphabet, Typo-Illustration, 2024,
Manuel Viergutz, www.TypoGraphicDesign.de

Manuel Viergutz is a
Graphic-Designer,
Type-Designer &
Lettering-Artist based
in Berlin. Founder of
the Font-Foundry
TypoGraphicDesign.de

TYPODARIUM

September, 25th Thursday

नित्य रञ्जना

Nithya Ranjana (Script-Ranjana), Script, 2024
Tathagata Biswas, Noopur Datye, www.ektype.in

|| नयाल ताया यलिक ||

नवारी ताया ख्वे लिपिदक्मा लाख्ग्रा।
ती मध्ये यम्ल लिपिदक नञ्जना लिपि,
यबलित, वाज्रि, तुर्डिमाल हन।
यी सर्वे लिपिदक व्ववास दायोतया
लाख्ग्रन, तब क्वसाझन तन माहिवास
तल लाख्ग्रा। यी सर्वे लिपिमा स्वरमाला
व व्यञ्जनमाला गरी हनु यकबक
यक्वनदक हन।✳✳✳

TYPODARIUM

September

26

Friday

Bulbia

Bulbia, Display, 2023,
Michael Parson, www.typogama.com

Bulbia
is a single weight,
display typeface

❧

September

Saturday

Teramo

Teramo, Variable Serif, 2020,
Roch Modrzejewski, www.rohhtype.com

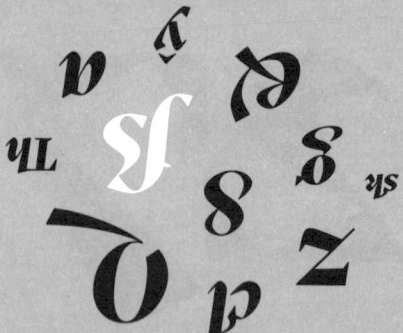

September

Czech Statehood Day (CZ)

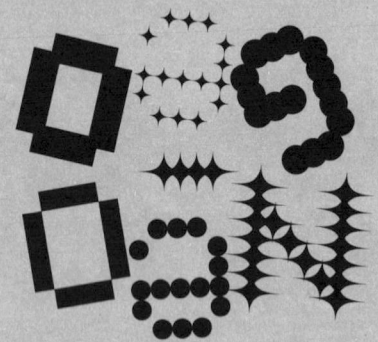

NEO-GEO

Neo-Geo, Variable Display, 2023,
David Šulc, www.wtypefoundry.com

September

29

Monday

Grantig

Grantig, Slab, 2023,
Julien Fincker, www.julienfincker.com

Slant
abcdefghijklmn
opqrstuvwxyz
ABCDEFGHIJKLMN
OPQRSTUVWXYZ
0123456789 @?!
Backslant

TYPODARIUM

September

30

Tuesday

Allamare

Allamare, Script, 2021,
Zakhar Yaschin, www.paratype.com/fonts/zy/allamare

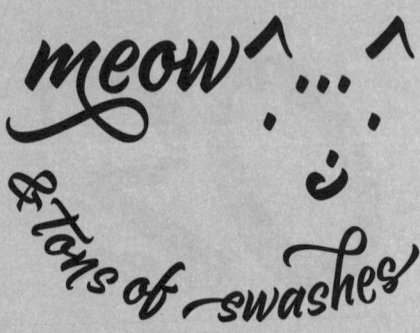

meow^...^ & tons of swashes

TYPODARIUM

OCTOBER

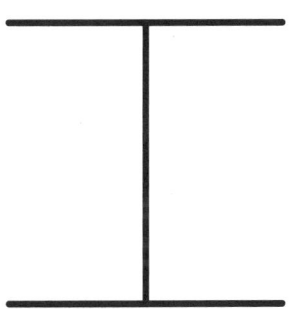

1

National Day (CN)

WEDNESDAY

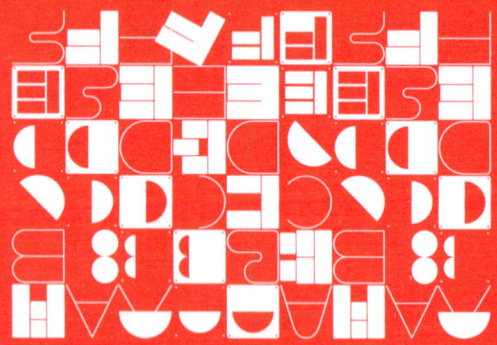

TpDonutShop, Display, 2024,
Martin Lorenz, www.twopoints.net

TP DONUT SHOP

OCTOBER

2

Gandhi Jayanti (IN)

Thursday

Fugua

Fugua Slab, 2024,
Jon Young, www.garagefonts.com

Monochromatic	Unconstitutional
Insurmountably	Openmindedness
Heartsearching	Archaeologically
Supernumerary	Hypochondriacal
Airconditioner	Superintendents
Everincreasing	Incommunicable
Disassociating	Timeconsuming
Metalinguistic	Underpopulation
Reciprocation	Quintessentially
Thoroughbred	Indiscriminately

October

German Unity Day (DE), National Foundation Day (KR)

REZAK

Rezak, Text & Display, 2022.
Anya Danilova, www.type-together.com/rezak-font

A jaunty, dynamic type family 🗿 that 🗿 *stretches beyond one specific* 🗿 font category and use.

TYPODARIUM

OCTOBER

4

Saturday

Verso

Italic

Regular

Solfa Sans, 2023,
Catarina Vaz & Rui Abreu, www.r-typography.com

SOLFA

October

Republic Day (PT), Chuseok (Korean Thanksgiving Day) (KR)

Plage

Plage, Sans, 2021,
Bouk Ra, www.lift-type.fr

Plage Family
— 6 Styles —
A Large Set of
Ligatures &
Alternates

TYPODARIUM

October

6

Chuseok (Korean Thanksgiving Day) (KR),
Mid-Autumn Festival (CN, VN)

Monday

SUB-TOPICS
DEVELOPER
CP/M-8000
FILMSTOCK

Image Future, Sans, 2024,
Guillaume Goron, www.productiontype.com

Image Future

October

7

Chuseok (Korean Thanksgiving Day) (KR)

Tuesday

POPCORN CRISPY

TT Trailers, Display Sans, 2022,
TypeType Foundry, www.typetype.org

TT Trailers

OCTOBER

WEDNESDAY

KTT GRAYZONE JANUS

KTT Grayzone Janus, Display, 2024,
Youl Joe & Heejae Yang, www.ktowntype.com

IT REPRESENTS A
HYBRID CONCEPT
OF BLACK AND
WHITE, DUALITY,
AND UNCERTAINTY.

TYPODARIUM

October

9

Hangeul Day (KR)

Thursday

„May *serifs* always line your path and contrast light your day."

LD Elly, Serif, 2024.
Bente Baseler, www.Lazydogs.de

LD Elly

October

10

Friday

Registering

conversation

Philosophical

sociolinguistics

Consists of grammar

Cosimo Lorenzo Pancini, Andrea Tartarelli, www.zetafonts.com
Dialogue, Serif, 2023,

Dialogue

October

11

Saturday

Dani

Dani, Variable Sans & Text, 2024,
Jo De Baerdemaeker, www.studiotype.be

Welcome to Dani, a unique sans
serif type revival that originates
from the Brussels-based
type foundry of Van Loey-Nouri.

Dani is part of 'Typo Belgïque',
a design & research project that
breathes new life into Belgium's
historical typeface families.

October

Day of Respect for Cultural Diversity (AR),
Our Lady of Aparecida (BR), National Day of Spain (SP)

Dudler

Dudler, Display, 2022,
Franziska Weitgruber, www.franziskaweitgruber.com

Environment
Perpendicular
construction and maintanance

TYPODARIUM

October

13

Thanksgiving Day (CA), Health and Sports Day (JP),
Columbus Day (USA, CO)

Monday

19th century to early 20th

GROTESQUE

modernity or minimalism

awesome

lower – resolution digital displays

Quat, Sans Serif, 2019,
Anji Dimitrova, www.anjidimitrova.com

Quat

OCTOBER

14

TUESDAY

TYPODARIUM

GRAZ GRAZ GRAZ GRAZ
SCHAUSPIELHAUS
GRAZ GRAZ GRAZ GRAZ
SCHAUSPIELHAUS
GRAZ GRAZ GRAZ GRAZ
SCHAUSPIELHAUS

Ensemble Mono, Mono, 2023,
Mona Franz, www.justyourtype.de

ENSEMBLE MONO

October

15

Wednesday

Palast

Palast, Serif, 2021,
Hannes von Döhren & Bernd Volmer, www.hvdfonts.com

A *high* CONTRAST TYPE SYSTEM *with* *three* OPTICAL SIZES.

✸

Each FAMILY WITH 12 STYLES.

TYPODARIUM

October

16

Thursday

Aa Bb Cc Dd Ee
Ff Gg Hh Ii Jj Kk
Ll Mm Nn Oo Pp
Qq Rr Ss Tt Uu Vv
Ww Xx Yy Zz

Ziza Contrast, Display, 2018.
Mark van Wageningen, Novo Typo, www.novotypo.nl

Ziza Contrast

OCTOBER

17

Friday

Megato

Megato, Sans, 2022,
Andreas Seidel, www.astype.de, fontstore.astype.com

Megato - a typeface with a distinct industrial vibe that is continually un- der development. Supporting Cyrillic Кириллица, Greek Ελληνική, Hebrew ת‎ברית, Japanese Hiragana ひらがな, Katakana カタカナ and a growing list of Kanji 漢字.

※ ASTYPE│アシ活字体 ※

TYPODARIUM

October

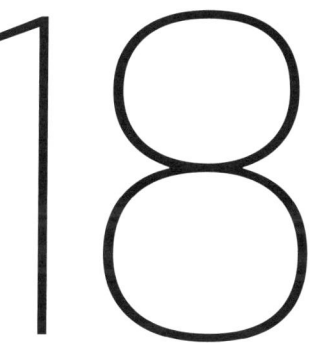

Saturday

UPDATE

Update, Sans, 2024,
Ricardo Santos, www.vanarchive.com

Broadcasting

Variety of types of information can be transmitted

Electric and Manufacturing Company

Digital Modulation

Extremely high frequency

Downlink signal to a rooftop satellite dish antenna

TYPODARIUM

OCTOBER

19

SUNDAY

ADORABLY

IKEBANA

SMOOTHIE

Gizela, Display, 2021,
Alja Herlah, www.type-salon.com

GIZELA

October

20

Vietnamese Women's Day (VN), Deepavali (MY)

Monday

Right Grotesk *Mono*

Right Grotesk Mono, Variable Sans, 2023,
Alex Slobzheninov, www.slobzheninov.com

Gøre *Visziņkārīgākais*

Förmå **Időszerűtlenség**

Għażel *Mißverständnis*

Démâter Nedorečenošću

Krężołek *Slovíčkářský*

Exposiçaõ Pääkäyttäjä

Tölvufræði *Rafraîchir*

TYPODARIUM

OCTOBER

21

Diwali (IN)

TUESDAY

SIROKO

Siroko, Sans, 2024,
Bouk Ra, www.bouk.work

*

{ Journée Ensoleillée }

VENT DOUX & APAISANT

~

TYPODARIUM

October

22

Wednesday

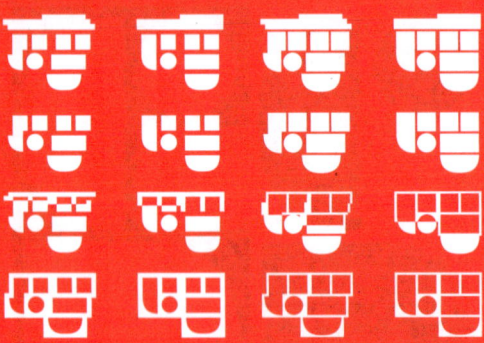

Trafarett, Variable Display, 2023,
Almur Täkk, www.typokompanii.com

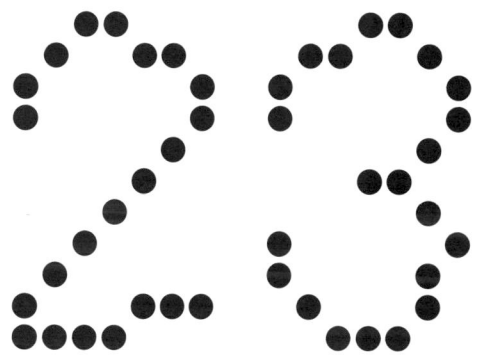

OCTOBER

23

THURSDAY

Locher Variable, 2025,
Lina Kaltenberg, www.lina-kaltenberg.de

LOCHER VARIABLE

October

24

Friday

Basketball
Frisbee
Hula Hoop
Donut
Pancake

Moderat Rounded, Sans, 2024,
tightype, www.tightype.com

Moderat Rounded

S like Scorpius
24 October - 22 November

Zodiac Alphabet

Zodiac Alphabet, Typo-Illustration, 2024,
Manuel Viergutz, www.TypoGraphicDesign.de

Manuel Viergutz is a Graphic-Designer, Type-Designer & Lettering-Artist based in Berlin. Founder of the Font-Foundry TypoGraphicDesign.de

TYPODARIUM

October

25

Saturday

Commodore

Commodore, Mono Serif, 2023,
Hugues Gentile, www.productiontype.com

ATMOSPHERIC PRESSURE	RHINELAND-PALATINATE
FERMIONIC CONDENSATE	JOHN SHEPHERD-BARRON
BEHAVIORAL NEUROLOGY	CLARENDON LABORATORY
CHALLENGE HYPOTHESIS	PETER MAXWELL DAVIES
INTELLECTUAL CAPITAL	ALFRED LORD TENNYSON
TRANSVERSE ARROWHEAD	MULTIPLE PERSPECTIVE
PIEZOELECTRIC EFFECT	ZOSIMOS OF PANOPOLIS
ARISTARCHUS OF SAMOS	HELENA BONHAM CARTER
CAUSEWAYED ENCLOSURE	OVERSEAS TERRITORIES
SCOTTISH RENAISSANCE	PHILOSOPHY OF DESIGN
BASIC OXYGEN PROCESS	STATISTICAL GRAPHICS
CLASSICAL DEMOGRAPHY	BELL ROCK LIGHTHOUSE

26

National Day (AT)

Sunday

Partner

Partner, Variable, 2024,
Jule Hägele, www.whatsyourtype.de

Partner is a variable
typeface which contains
five different axes.

Find and download
your *perfect*
partner today
♡

TYPODARIUM

OCTOBER

Monday

27

الاثنين

GROSSER¹⁰

Grosser 10, Display, 2024,
Leo Colalillo, www.leocolalillo.com

INSPIRED BY NORTHERN
EUROPEAN MODERN
ARCHITECTURE, IN ITS **10™**
ANNIVERSARY EDITION, WITH
NEW GLYPHS AND THE ADDITION
OF THE **ARABIC** ALPHABET

× **GEOMETRICALLY**
× **RUMFREDILEGT**
× **ГЕОМЕТРИЧЕСКИЙ**
× **الكسرة**

{{(@LFE*gª£¤€%.77R§ñ*‡πŒ))}}

TYPODARIUM

October

28

Ochi Day (GR)

Tuesday

Epilox

Epsilon, Sans, 2021,
Deni Anggara, www.formatypefoundry.com

♪ Maximum of Song
⊕ (WORLD EYE) ∞
"A fun Grafique" ⊚
↗ It's New 👾 Club 📷
* * *
Aa Aa Aa Aa Aa

October

29

Republic Day (TR), Double Ninth Festival (CN)

Wednesday

Rationalist design

Gestalt principles

MODERNITY

BAUHAUS *The grid organises space*

Arbale, Sans, 2023,
Jean François Porchez, www.typofonderie.com

Arbale

October

30

THURSDAY

texture

sharp

slab

fashionable

Dockland, Variable Slab, 2023,
Tom Holloway, www.TypeMates.com

Dockland

October

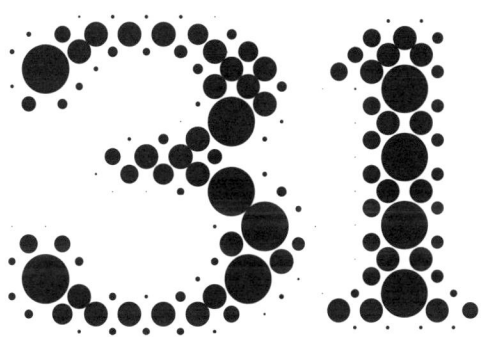

Reformation Day (SI)

Friday

RR-Pecas

RR-Pecas, Display, 2025.
Rafael Ramírez Lozano, Baj1otype, www.baj1otype.com

«We are» FONTS

ÁBCDEFGHIJKLMN
ÑOPQRSTUVWXYZ
abcdefghijklmnñopqrstuvwxyz
1234567890()[]|!¡¿?&/=<>«»:;,."...

TYPODARIUM

NOVEMBER

All Saints' Day

SATURDAY

GTF MYCENA

GTF Mycena, Display, 2023,
Good Type Foundry, www.goodtypefoundry.com

ABCDEFG
HIJKLMNO
PQRSTUV
WXYZ

TYPODARIUM

NOVEMBER

All Souls' Day

BRIAR DISPLAY

Briar Display, 2020.
Barrett Reid-Maroney, www.barrettrm.com

ABCDEF
GHIJKLM
NOPQR
STUVWXYZ

November

3

Culture Day (JP)

Monday

Silverio

Silverio, Display, 2024,
Gabriel Pulpo, www.pulpo.mx

"One can perfectly well philosophize while cooking supper."

—Juana Inés de la Cruz

TYPODARIUM

NOVEMBER

Day of National Unity (RU)

TUESDAY

Jeffrey Zeldman

"DON'T WORRY ABOUT PEOPLE STEALING IDEAS, WORRY ABOUT THE DAY THEY STOP..."

André Toet, www.antretoet.com
Herengracht, Display, 2022.

HERENGRACHT

November

5

Wednesday

Elegant but Friendly

Text & Headlines • Shake it out Baby!

Wicked Ways

VIENNA WAITS FOR YOU

elegant@mail.com

Alive since 1984/Oliva Street 255

HIGH CONTRAST

Ollin, Display Serif, 2024,
Dafne Martínez, www.tipastype.com

Ollin

November

Thursday

Sharp Serif

Sharp Serif, Serif, 2024, Lucas Sharp & Connor Davenport,
Jovana Jocić, Lena Le Pommelet & My-Lan Thuong, www.sharptype.co

Aries ♈
Taurus ♉
Gemini ♊
Cancer ♋
Leo ♌
Virgo ♍

Libra ♎
Scorpio ♏
Sagittarius ♐
Capricorn ♑
Aquarius ♒
Pisces ♓

NOVEMBER

FRIDAY

IAGO

Iago, Serif, 2024,
Bouk Ra, https://bouk.work

PHANTOM MIME SORCERER

November

8

Saturday

HAL Four Grotesk (white cube)

HAL Four Grotesk (white cube), Sans, 2023,
HAL Typefaces, type.hanli.eu

Rijksmuseum Gagosian
MoMA Tate Prado
Saatchi Palais de Tokyo
Louisiana Perrotin
Guggenheim Kulturforum
Sprüth Magers
Thaddaeus Ropac HKW
Hauser & Würth

TYPODARIUM

November

9

sunday

No. 43, Display, 2023,
Road to Venice Type, www.r-vtype.com

giving freedom
& independency

November

10

Monday

PP Pangaia

PP Pangaia, Serif, 2023, Samuel Salminen, Mat Desjardins &
Francesca Bolognini, www.pangrampangram.com

Whole Earth

Catalogue

Polar Quórum

Gondwana

Microplastics

TYPODARIUM

NOVEMBER

Armistice Day (BE, FR), Veterans Day (USA),
Remembrance Day (CA), Independence Day (PL),
Independence of Cartagena (CO)

TUESDAY

Questions
Firebreak
Objective
Resonates
Gymnasia

Expromt Slab, 2020-ongoing,
Kateryna Korolevtseva, www.korolevtseva.com

Expromt

November

12

Wednesday

Finlay

Finlay, Sans Script, 2023,
Martin Wenzel, supertype®, www.supertype.de/fonts/finlay

Aa Bb Cc Dd Ee Ff Gg Hh Ii Jj
Kk Ll Mm Nn Oo Pp Qq Rr Ss Tt
Uu Vv Ww Xx Yy Zz · 12 34 56
78 90 → €¥ #£ &@ ?! 12 ¾ ·] })

* * *

Light SemiLight Regular
Medium **Bold** **ExtraBold** **Black**

* * *

Finlay · Finlay · FINLAY

TYPODARIUM

November

13

Thursday

Light Sans	Light Classic	Light Decor
Regular Sans	Regular Classic	Regular Decor
Medium Sans	Medium Classic	Medium Decor
Bold Sans	Bold Classic	Bold Decor
Black Sans	Black Classic	Black Decor

Notice Sans
Notice Classic
Notice Decor

EK Notice, Sans, 2024,
Erkin Karamemet, www.karamemet.com

EK Notice

November

14

Friday

Strong Character
Grotesque Sans
Typeshop Workhorse
Harmonious Family
19th Century Forms
Industrial Personality

Foundry Kingdom, Sans, 2024,
David Quay, Stuart de Rozatio, www.thefoundrytypes.com

Foundry Kingdom

November

15

Republic Proclamation Day (BR)

Saturday

Muoto Mono

Muoto Mono, Mono, 2023,
Matthieu Cortat, www.205.tf

Architect
Rational
Buildings
Practice
Designers
Slowness

TYPODARIUM

November

16

Sunday

Kurvatuur

Kurvatuur, Variable Display, 2024,
Aimur Takk, www.typokompanii.com

TYPODARIUM

November

17

Revolution Day (MX),
Struggle for Freedom and Democracy Day (CZ)

Monday

8. **Aeonik Condensed Black**
7. **Aeonik Condensed Bold**
6. Aeonik Condensed SemiBold
5. Aeonik Condensed Medium
4. Aeonik Condensed Regular
3. Aeonik Condensed Light
2. Aeonik Condensed Thin
1. Aeonik Condensed Air

Aeonik Condensed, Sans, 2024,
Mark Bloom, www.cotypefoundry.com

Aeonik Condensed

November

18

Tuesday

Carica, Display, 2023,
Anita Jürgeleit, www.typethis.studio

Carica

November

Wednesday

Loyle Flex, Display, 2024,
Martinus Klinksik, www.martinusklinksik.de

Loyle Flex

November

20

National Sovereignty Day (AR)

Thursday

The Crown
The Regalia
The Queen

LDN Clerkenwell Script, 2023,
Paul Harpin, Londontype.co.uk

Clerkenwell Script

November

21

Friday

Vandertak

Vandertak, Display, 2022,
Pieter van Rosmalen, www.caketype.com

Emendations	Ягломерація
Tortoiseshell	Ліхтенштейн
Cooperatives	Невідкладна
Troublesome	Одноименній
Recognisable	Відображення
Undissipated	Експлуатація
Conspirators	Кондиціонер

TYPODARIUM

November

22

Lebanese Independence Day (LB)

Saturday

Hollyday

Hollyday, Sans, 2015,
Márcio Duarte, Sea Types, www.peji.com.br

Hollyday is designed to be practical for use of **texts and titles.** Ideal for all applications.

Light, Regular & **Bold**

TYPODARIUM

S like Sagittarius
23 November - 21 December

Zodiac Alphabet

Zodiac Alphabet, Typo-Illustration, 2024,
Manuel Viergutz, www.TypoGraphicDesign.de

**Manuel Viergutz is a
Graphic-Designer,
Type-Designer &
Lettering-Artist based
in Berlin. Founder of
the Font-Foundry
TypoGraphicDesign.de**

November

23

Labour Thanksgiving Day (JP)

Sunday

MANGROVE

Mangrove, Sans & Script, 2023,
Sam Parrett, www.setsailstudios.com

A MIXABLE SANS & SCRIPT FONT DUO

TYPODARIUM

November

24

Monday

TYPODARIUM

6 weights, 12 styles
Latin & Cyrillic

Poster
Extrabold
Bold
Medium
Regular
Light

Poster
Extrabold
Bold
Medium
Regular
Light

Oceanic Gothic, Sans, 2023,
Interval Type, www.intervaltype.com

Oceanic Gothic

November

25

TUESDAY

Ltt:Recoleta

Ltt:Recoleta, Display, 2023,
Latinotype Team & Jorge Cisterna, www.latinotype.com

Pink juice: We're Up All Night To Get Funky.

Daft Punk–Get Lucky
(ft. P. Williams & Nile Rodgers)

TYPODARIUM

November

26

Wednesday

The time of year is upon us to indulge in boundless consumption — err, I meant compassion.

Seeboh, Display, 2024,
David Henni Wiesner, www.davidwiesner.de

Seeboh_V2

NOVEMBER

27

Thanksgiving Day (USA)

THURSDAY

MONOPOL KOMPAKT

Monopol Kompakt, Display, 2020,
Nguyen Gobber, www.nguyengobber.com

FUNKY SLOTHS GROOVING WITH MONKEYS & PARROTS IN THE JUNGLE

TYPODARIUM

November

28

Friday

AáBbŔ(Đěťuhiı)Ga@H3:№

Non Bureau, Sans, 2023,
Jona Saucedo, www.nonfoundry.com

Non Bureau

November

29

Saturday

New Nord

New Nord, Sans, 2023,
Botio Nikoltchev, www.lettersoup.de

Adventure
Prints & Objects
innovating beyond conventional
Breathtaking
22 Sep – 05 Oct 1985

TYPODARIUM

NOVEMBER

30

SUNDAY

ABC

Contrast Sans, Display, 2024,
Manuel Viergutz, www.TypographicDesign.de

CONTRAST SANS

ディセンバー

December, 1th Monday

Restoration of Independence (PT), National Day (RO)

ビーディーワカリマセン

BD Wakarimasen, Japanese Display, 2011/2023,
Lopetz, Büro Destruct, www.typedifferent.com

アァイィウゥエェオォカヮガキギ
クグケゲコゴサザシジスズセゼソゾタダ
チヂツッヅテデトドナニヌネノハバパヒビピフブ
プヘベペホボポマミムメモヤャユュヨョラ
リルレロワヮヲンヴ゛゜ー—
ヽ!?()／¥(),「」

ワカリマセン
Japanese
ONRY!

TYPODARIUM

December

Tuesday

OTC Textura

OTC Textura, Display, 2024,
Ograda Type Company, www.ograda.co

December

Wednesday

ROKHA

Rokha, Serif, 2023,
Gaspar Muñoz & Patricio Gonzalez, www.wtypefoundry.com

¶Dark Dog Gold Teeth
«Apologia de Lucifer»
Copperplate Gothic ④
⊹A͞V. Santa Rosa 01:25⊹
THE NIGHTMARES
Tales From The Cript
✠

TYPODARIUM

DECEMBER

4

THURSDAY

FASHiON EXPERiMENT

Fashion Experiment, Script, 2023,

Gulya Yeap, www.peachcreme.com

PEACHCREME'S DISPLAY-ISH FONT
ON STEROIDS, WITH
FANCY-SCHMANCY LIGATURES AND
ALTERNATES THAT'LL HAVE
vonr2 TEXT FLEXING ON SOME BASIC
DESIGNS out THERE

TYPODARIUM

December

5

Friday

BH Sans

BH Sans, Sans, 2024,
Michael Chereda, www.behance.net/brightheadstudio

BH Sans

Is a modern representative of the
grotesque genre, inspired by early
20th century drawings. It is a utilitarian
font family with a focus on clarity and
simplicity, and a modernist design.

The font was created for the internal
needs of our studio, but is now
available to a wide range of users.

TYPODARIUM

DECEMBER

Constitution Day (ES)

Saturday

I put ketchup on my slice of pizza and eat it like a taco.

Gurky Grotesque, Sans, 2024,
Hannes von Döhren, www.hvdfonts.com

Gurky Grotesque

December

Sunday

Marbla

Marbla, Variable, 2023,
Katharina Gresch, www.marbla.de

simple

funky

quickly

weird

smooth

December

8

Immaculate Conception

Monday

BLAST

Blast, Variable Sans, 2024,
Lucas Guizetti, www.lucasguizetti.cargo.site

Wind speed: BEAUFORT SCALE

Francis Beaufort (1774–1857)

203 km/h; *169 PS!*

*(Hydrographer)

December

Tuesday

NaR standa for not-a-Revival

NaR Partition, Display, 2025,
Đông-Trực, www.instagram.com/do_ngtruc/

nar Partition

DEC*EM*BER

Wed*NES*day

GLOBE

and products all around the

HTM_BICYCLES

can be seen in real life on

the "HUNDRED"

Hundred, Sans, 2023,
Jörg Walter, www.groupe-dejour.de

HUNDRED_BOLD_ITALIC

December

11

Thursday

· 0 1 2 3 4 5 6 7 8 9 0 1 2 3 4 ·

Elaborate
and cool.
You got it!

0 1 2 3 4 5 6 7 8

0 1 2 3 4 5 6 7 8

· 0 1 2 3 4 5 6 7 8 9 0 1 2 3 4 ·

Tandem Slab, Slab, 2024,
Kaja Stojewska & Paul Hanslow, www.tandemtype.co

Tandem Slab

DECEMBER

FRIDAY

EIGHTY DAYS

SPIRIT AND THE TRAVELING INSTINCT

ROADTRIP

AROUND THE WORLD

VACANCES

AW Conqueror Caps, Display, 2022,
Jean François Porchez, www.typofonderie.com

AW CONQUEROR CAPS

DECEMBER

13

Saturday

The Rage

Kill for Love

2012

Chromatics

Category, Sans, 2023,
VJType, www.vj-type.com

Category

December

14

Sunday

PROUD!

LOUD!

BOLD!

Edie and Eddy, Variable Serif, 2022.
Lisa Fischbach, www.TypeMates.com

Edie & Eddy

December

15

Monday

Archive Grotesk Mono

Archive Grotesk Mono, Mono Sans, 2024,
Christian Gruber, www.scifipoetry.de

text-align:
center
¡important;

December

16

Tuesday

Antiqua

Antiqua, Serif, 2024,
Trifon Andreev, www.trifonandreev.com

Buchdruckerkunst
sketches at Carnac
(Brittany) in 1834
neoclassical eleganza
хуманистичен

TYPODARIUM

December

17

wednesday

0123456789 !?

Aa Bb Cc Dd Ee
Ff Gg Hh Ii Jj Kk
Ll Mm Nn Oo Pp
Qq Rr Ss Tt Uu
Vv Ww Xx Yy Zz

Vivienne, Display, 2023,
Tobias Holzmann, www.tobiasholzmann.com

Vivienne

DECEMBER 십이 월

Thursday 목요일

★ Festival of Lights ★

빛의 축제

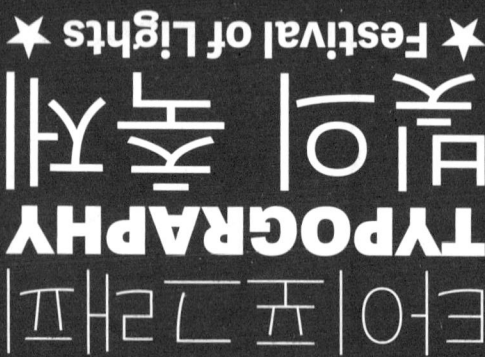

TYPOGRAPHY

타이포그래피

Adelle Sans Korean, 2023, Choron Kim & Changseop Im.
www.type-together.com/adelle-sans-korean-font

Adelle Sans Korean

December

19

Friday

Reading Hieroglyphs

DJOSER PYRAMID

Tulunid Era (868–905)

Great Ptolemaic Queen

"MURDER ON THE NILE"

PHARAON & MEMPHIS

Pow Alara, Display Sans, 2024,
Léo Guibert, www.proof-of-words.com

PoW Alara

December

20

Saturday

Breakfast

magazine ~

anagrammatizing

Natural feeling

American photojournalist

Cosimo Lorenzo Pancini & Andrea Tartarelli, www.zetafonts.com
Evans, Serif, 2023.

Evans

December

21

Sunday

WATERCOLOR? OIL
Acrylic? charcoal?
Crayon, gouache!

Intern Color Sans, 2024,
İbrahim Kaçtıoğlu & Doğukan Karapınar, www.elementtype.co

INTERN

C like Capricorn
22 December - 20 January

Zodiac Alphabet

Zodiac Alphabet, Typo-Illustration, 2024,
Manuel Viergutz, www.TypoGraphicDesign.de

Manuel Viergutz is a
Graphic-Designer,
Type-Designer &
Lettering-Artist based
in Berlin. Founder of
the Font-Foundry
TypoGraphicDesign.de

TYPODARIUM

December

22

Monday

TYPODARIUM

BERGMAN
WENDERS
CHRYSSA
PICTONS

TBD WTF, Display, 2024,
The Birthaus Design, www.thebirthausdesign.com

TBD WTF

ديسمبر

December, 23th Tuesday

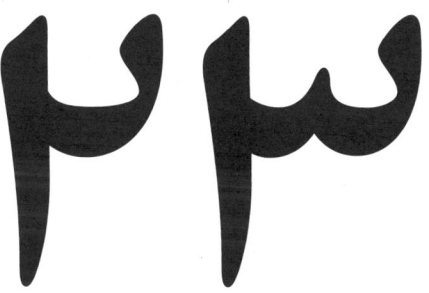

الثلاثاء

F37 Bobby العربية

F37 Bobby Arabic, Serif, 2023.
F37 Foundry, www.f37foundry.com

F37 Bobby هو خط عنوان ودود و دافئ مع لمسة هندسية خفية

Light *Italic* Regular *Italic* Bold *Italic*
٠١٢٣٤٥٦٧٨٩ .,:" ([{!?@£$%&}])

TYPODARIUM

December

24

Wednesday

Schaffer Ribbon

Schaffer Ribbon, Display, 2023,
Mona Franz, www.justyourtype.de

»Ohhhhh,
it's the most
wonderful time of
the year!«

TYPODARIUM

DECEMBER

Christmas Day

THURSDAY

1234567890

ABCDEFGHIJ
KLMNOPQRS
TUVWXYZ

Calix, Display, 2024,
Marja Bos & Rachelle Jeurling, www.studioneon.nl

CALIX

December

26

St. Stephen's Day (AT), Boxing Day

Friday

Ritual Mono

Ritual Mono, VarIable Mono, 2023,
Lukas Schneider, www.revolvertype.com

Airport→Access

Gate	Board Time	Seat
A14	10:45	C-068

Terminal→Route

123 ☀ 🌐 ✿ 67 ←↓→↑ 89

Public→Transit

TYPODARIUM

DECEMBER

27

SATURDAY

MORTA

Morta, Script, 2023.
Michael Rafailyk, www.michaelrafailyk.com

A HANDWRITTEN UNICASE
TYPEFACE WITH A SLIGHT
CALLIGRAPHIC INFLUENCE.
ITS DESIGN, LIKE A
CENTURIES-OLD COLD DARK
STONES, HAS CARVED EDGES
AND POLISHED CORNERS.

December

28

Sunday

BVH Bart Display

BVH Bart Display, Display, 2022, André Baldinger & Toan Vu-Huu, Jimmy Le Guennec, Fanny Hameline, www.bvhtype.com

AaBbCcDdEeFfGgHhIiJjKkLlMm
NnOoPpQqRrSsTtUuVvWwXx
YyZz 0123456789 ..;:... !?¿'""''@

Bart Display-Regular

Bart Display-Italic

Bart Display-Medium

Bart Display-Medium Italic

Bart Display-Bold

Bart Display-Bold Italic

Bart Display-Heavy

Bart Display-Heavy Italic

TYPODARIUM

December

29

Monday

sonson

Sonson, Sans, 2024,
Jong·Beom Kim, www.nodetonode.kr

Mug Cup
Depression
Tray
Candle
Ornaments

TYPODARIUM

December

Tuesday

Gargoyles

Astonishing

Architecture

Expressive

Eckhart, Didone Serif & color font, 2019,
Roch Modrzejewski, www.rohhtype.com

Eckhart

December

31

Wednesday

TYPODARIUM

TT Travels Next, Display Sans, 2021,
TypeType Foundry, www.typetype.org

TT Travels Next

Thank you

205TF, 29LT, 3type, A. Alameddine, A. Korolkova, A. Lubovenko,
Adam Greasley, Aimur Takk, Alanna Munro, Alex Bossi,
Alex Slobzheninov, Alexander Kapusta, Alexander Rütten,
Alexander Wright, Alexandre Bassi, Alfonso García, Alja Herlah,
Alyona Korysta, Anagha Narayanan, André Baldinger, André Toet,
Andrea Leksen, Andrea Tartarelli, Andreas Seidel, Andreas Uebele,
Andree Paat, Andrei Ograd, Ani Dimitrova, Anita Jürgeleit,
Antipixel Type Studio, Anya Danilova, Ariel Brandolini,
Art Grootfontein, Arthur Schwarz, Astype, Autograph, BajioType,
Barrett, Reid-Maroney, BB-Bureau, Benedict Fromme,
Benjamin Paul Knopper, Benoît Bodhuin, Bente Baseler,
Bernd Volmer, Black Foundry, Blaze Type, Bonez Designz,
Botio Nikoltchev, Bouk Ra, Brave Type, Bureau Brut, Büro Destruct,
Cadson Demak, Cake Type, Calvin Kwok, Cape Arcona Type Foundry,
CAST Foundry, Catarina Vaz, Changseop Im, Charlene Sepentzis,
Choron Kim, Christian Gruber, Christian Lindermann, Christoph
Ulherr, Colt Type Co, Connor Davenport, Contextype, Corradine
Fonts, Cosimo Lorenzo Pancini, CoType Foundry, Cris Hernández,
D. Goloub, Dafne Martínez, David Gobber, David Henni Wiesner,
David Quay, David Súid, Debora Steffen, Deni Anggara, Design
Associati, Diego Aravena Silo, Dogukan Karapınar, Đông-Trúc
Nguyen, Egor Belozerov, Ek Type, Element Type, Elena Schönsee,
Emerson Eller, Emmanuel Besse, Emphase, Erkin Karamemet,
Ewen Prigent, F37 Foundry, Fabian Dornhecker, Fabian Fohrer,

And you

Fabrizio Falcone, Fang-Ping Lin, Fanny Hamelin, Felix Braden,
Felix Fissenewert, Felix Pfäffli, Filippo Saltuma, Florian Fecher,
Francesca Bolognini, Francesco Canovaro, Franziska Weitgruber,
Frederick Wiltshire, Frederico Parra Barrios, Frederik Merkel,
G-Type, Gabriel Pulpo, Gabriel Richter, Gaëtan Baehr, Garage
Fonts, Gaspar Muñoz, Good Type Foundry, Gregor Maria Sahl,
Groupe Dejour, Guillaume Goron, Gulya Yeap, Hannes von Döhren,
Hanspeter Lobis, Hanzer Liccini, Heejae Yang, Hoang Nguyen,
Hugues Gentil, Hunger & Koch, HvD fonts, I Love Typography,
İbrahim Kaçıoğlu, In-House, Interval Type, Jacob Wise, Jakob
Fangmeier, Jakob Runge, Jamie Clarke Type, Jan Eloy Gabriel,
Jan Tonellato, Jan Weidemüller, Jasper Nijssen, Jean François
Porchez, Jérémie Hornus, Jimmy Le Guennec, Jo De Baerdemaeker,
Joachim Vu, Joe Graham, John Vargas Beltrán, Jon Young,
Jona Saucedo, Jong-Beom Kim, Jörg Walter, Jorge Cisterna, José
Carratalá, José Scaglione, Jovana Jocic, Jozef Ondrík, Jule Hägele,
Julia Hell, Julia Martínez Diana, Julien Fincker, Just Your Type,
K Town Type, K. Radoeva, KaamKaaj, Kaja Słojewska, Kateryna
Korolevtseva, Katharina Gresch, Katharina Valkenkamp,
Kazuhiro Yamada, Kilo Peng, Kostas Bartsokas, Krista Likar,
Krista Radoeva, Kwangmoo Lee, La Bolde Vita, Latino Type,
Laura Meseguer, Lea Marie Schulz, Léna Le Pommelet, Lena Schmidt,
Leo Colalillo, Léo Guibert, Leonhard Katschner, Leopoldo Leal,
Lettersoup, Li Yang, Li Zhijian, Life Type, Lina Kaltenberg,

And you

Linus Knappe, Lisa Drös, Lisa Fischbach, Lisa Semrau, London Type Foundry, Lorenz Gianfreda, Lucas Descroix, Lucas Guizetti, Lucas Sharp, Luciano Vergara, Lukas Schneider, Lukas Ulonska, Maël Bächthold, Maha Akl, Maja Rüffer, makes no semse, Manuel Corradine, Manuel Viergutz, Mara Nolze, Márcio Duarte, Maria Bos, María Ramos, Marinus Klinksik, Mario De Libero, Mark Bloom, Mark van Wageningen, Markus Strümpel, Martin Lorenz, Martin Wenzel, Mat Desjardins, Matej Vojtuš, Mathew Prada, Matthieu Cortat, Mattia Luise, Max Esnée, Michael Chereda, Michael Parson, Michael Rafailyk, Mona Franz, Monika Gause, My-Lan Thuong, N. Nedashkovsky, Natalie Giesel, Néstor Rocha García, Nice to type you, Nick Cooke, NM Type, Noel Pretorius, Nolan Paparelli, Non Foundry, Noopur Datye, Novotypo, Ograda Type Company, Olivia Wood, pangram.pangram, PARATYPE, Pascal Zoghbi, Patricio Gonzalez, Paul Bokslag, Paul Eslage, Paul Hanslow, Paul Harpin, Peachcreme, Peter Korsman, Peter Malutzki, Philip Lammert, Pieter van Rosmalen, Production Type, Prof. Jürgen Huber, Proof of Words, R-Typography, Raban Ruddigkeit, Rachelle Jeuring, Radinal Riki Mutaqin, Rafael Ramirez Lozano, REALTYPE, RegularLines, Revolver Type, Ricardo Santos, Road to Venice Type, Robby Woodard, Robert Finkei, Robin Eberwein, Roch Modrzejewski, ROHH Type Foundry, Romain Diant, Romain Oudin, Roman Seban, Roman Wilhelm, Rui Abreu, Sam Parrett, Samuel Götschin, Samuel Salminen, Sandra García, Scribbletone,

And you

Sea Types, Sebastian Moock, Shahd El-Sabbagh, Sharp Type,
Shintaro Ajioka, Sidharth Jaishankar, Solenn Bordeau,
Song Yingming, Sophia Tai, Sou Magazine, Stefan Claudius,
Stuart de Rozario, Studio Feixen, Studio Neon, Supertype, T. Grace,
Tana Kosiyabong, TandemType, Taresh Vohra, Tathagata Biswas,
The Birthdays Design, The Foundry Types, Thomas Schostok,
Tien-Min Liao, Tighttype, Tipastype, Toan Vu-Huu, Tobias Holzmann,
Tom Holloway, Tomasz Pawluk, Trifon Andreev, Twopoints,
Tyler McFaul, Type Salon, Type Together, TypeMates,
TypeType, Typofonderie, Typogama, Typo Graphic Design, Typokompa-
nii, Ultra Kuhl, V. Evstafieva, Vectro Type, Veronika Burian,
Vibrant Types, Víctor Gómez, Victor Nübel,
Viktor Zumegen, VJ Type, W TYPE FOUNDRY, W. Crouwel, Wei-Yun Kan,
Xing Zhichao, Yarza Twins, Yesha Goshar, Youl Joe,
Zakhar Yaschin, Zeta Fonts, Zhan Goudong, Zusanna Gruszczynaska

Imprint

Edited by Lars Harmsen & Raban Ruddigkeit

Lars is a designer, typographer, and lecturer from Karlsruhe. He is creative director of the Melville Brand Design agency, editor of Slanted magazine and blog (www.slanted.de), founder of Volcano Type font-publishing house (www.volcano-type.de) and member of the ADC Germany. www.melvilledesign.de

Raban is a designer, editor & illustrator. After ten years as a graphic designer & another ten years in classical advertising, he has brought the strengths of both fields together in his own atelier in Berlin. More than 150 international awards, worldwide lectures & teachings are as much a part of his daily work as the development & editing of Freistil-The Book Of Illustrators, Typodarium & Photodarium (both with Lars Harmsen) as well as the Berlin Design Digest (with Robert Eysoldt). www.ruddigkeit.de

Hardie Grant

NORTH AMERICA

Art Direction, Curation & Cover Design: Julia Uplegger

She is a designer, typographer, type designer and
illustrator. She likes to think beyond the obvious
into the white space of creativity.
www.julia-uplegger.de

Originally published in 2024 by Verlag Hermann Schmidt
Karin & Bertram Schmidt-Friderichs, www.typografie.de

Published by Hardie Grant North America
Jenny Wapner, www.hardiegrantusa.com

Printed in Türkiye

TYPODARIUM